THE MULTINATIONAL TAKEDOWN OF AMERICA

AS A PRELUDE TO
BARACK OBAMA'S
DESIRE TO HAVE BEEN
THE NEXT
SECRETARY-GENERAL
OF THE UNITED NATIONS

GARY R. PATTERSON

outskirtspress

DENVER, COLORADO

Dedication

Elaine Patterson, the mother and grandmother of our three lovely daughters and five grandchildren. I will forever be beholden to Elaine for the inestimable love and devotion that she has bestowed upon all of them throughout her life.

Contents

Barack Obama's Desire and Intention to One Day Become the Secretary-General of the United Nations

> "(President Obama) does have one more campaign in him… he's now running to be the next Secretary-General of the United Nations. Now it ALL makes sense, A LOT OF SENSE.
> **Bookmark this. You read it here first."**
> (Note: Bold print and Caps emphasis added by *Redstate. com*)
> *RedState.com* – "Fecklessness Has Its Rewards: Barack Obama Will Be the Next United Nations Secretary-General" - March 17, 2014

Well…not exactly. In March 2011, clearly three years before the prediction of RedState.com (then-Editor: Erick Erickson, noted Conservative political commentator), this author made the original case as to Barack Obama's ultimate desire, after leaving the White House, of becoming the next Secretary-General of the United Nations in 2017. In 2011, this assertion was based precisely upon twelve major foreign policy positions and decisions President Obama had taken during just the first two years (2009-2010) of his presidency (See Listing of 12 Events and Decisions – beginning of Chapter 2).[1]

Moreover, as President, since 2010 virtually all subsequent major foreign policy decisions made during the course of Barack Obama's Presidency have only served to validate this assertion. Yet, after seven years of the Obama presidency, no one else (other than *Redstate.com* and this author) had postulated this theory. **But why?**

The Media's Blinded Mindset

> *"I don't understand. [President Obama] has completely horn-swoggled and tricked the American People and pushed through a deal [i.e. The Iran Nuclear Deal] that is going to jeopardize the entire future of the world. **Why? Why? Why is he doing this? And what is the [Presidential] legacy? The legacy here is a disaster."***
> Ben Stein, Noted Economist and Commentator – Criticizing the Iran Nuclear Deal – *Fox News - Cavuto on Business* – September 5, 2015

Ben Stein's exasperation as to President Obama's justification and motivation pertaining to the Iran Nuclear Deal was illustrative of many in the media - and not just Conservatives. However, the media are collectively blinded by the subliminal paradigm of thought that the accepted ultimate political "End Game" of any President of the United States is to be re-elected to a second term – typically connoting a successful presidency from a presidential legacy perspective. Game over. A President then retires, writes his multi-million dollar memoirs and chooses to serve in some philanthropic endeavor in retirement.

The media unconsciously accepts this to be the consensus successful destiny and Modus Operandi career path sought by all U.S. Presidents and former Presidents. *Thus, it is with this narrow, engrained mindset that virtually all political pundits, on both the left and right, are consequently at a loss to explain why President Obama has frequently taken U.S. foreign policy positions throughout his presidency that are diametrically opposed by a decided majority of the American People – typically, opposition ranging from 60%-70%* (i.e. 1. The Iran Nuclear Deal; 2. Opposing the Keystone Pipeline; 3. a Carbon Emissions Tax; 4. Amnesty for Illegals; 5. Closing GTMO and 6. Continually placating anti-sematic Muslim nations at the expense of Israel while publically rebuking Israeli Prime Minister Benjamin Netanyahu on more than one occasion).

However, when attempting to put a finger on his true motivation, what the media unconsciously failed to consider was the real possibility that a parallel purpose which would explain Barack Obama's actions in conducting U.S. foreign policy throughout his Presidency extended beyond just the end of his second term as President. **Consider: What if President Obama's paradigm is more than just a two-term Presidency?** What if President Obama wants more than that? What if, after serving out a two-term Presidency, Barack Obama has further political ambitions to one day become Secretary-General of the United Nations as well after leaving the White House? What if that is President Obama's paradigm and Modus Operandi that would explain his conduct of U.S. foreign policy?

Tracking Obama's Adoption and Adherence to U.N. Policy

Illustratively, even the mainstream media was perplexed as to why President Obama consciously, proactively and repeatedly insisted that the term, "Radical Islamic Terrorism," was a misnomer - having absolutely no connection to the Muslim religion – as the President believes it is merely a convenient pretext employed by otherwise demented secular Arab militia groups bent on somehow appearing legitimate in justifying their maniacal savagery throughout the world. However, is it not just as plausible that Obama's true tactical political intent is to *differentiate and distance himself personally from the perception worldwide of the mainstream of American thought* – in hopes of ingratiating himself in the future with those Muslim nations whose support, as a prerequisite, Obama must ultimately have to one day be elected as the United Nations Secretary-General.

Or, in February 2015, both sides of the political spectrum were left to wonder "out of where" do certain Obama Administration policy statements come from - like State Department Spokesperson Marie Harf declaring that 1) the root cause of terrorism was, in fact, poverty and joblessness and that 2) the United States bears a significant measure of responsibility to address and help solve the problem. Although, Ms. Harf's declaration was not at all "out of left field," but, rather, was taken directly out of the United Nations "handbook" and accepted as gospel and espoused by the Obama Administration.

However, Ms. Harf wasn't the first official in the Obama Administration to openly express the need for and responsibility of all nations, especially the United States, to address the true "root social causes" of terrorism. Indeed, it was President Obama himself at the United Nations in September 2014 (five months earlier) who declared *"We must work to address...the oppression, lack of opportunity, too often the hopelessness that can make some individuals susceptible to appeals of extremism and violence."*[2]

More importantly, note just how closely the statements of President Obama and State Department spokesperson Harf - about the root causes of terrorism - parallel the sentiment *initially expressed by the*

United Nations in a U.N. conference policy statement, dated June 13-14, 2013, (and over a year before Barack Obama's September 2014 statement quoted above):

1. "Among the many conditions that are conducive to the spread of terrorism, *the lack of economic opportunities* and the absence of balanced and sustainable development are particularly important."
   International Counter-Terrorism Focal Points Conference and addressing Conditions Conducive to the Spread of Terrorism and Promoting Regional Cooperation (Section III: Linkages between Development and Security – Page 3).

2. Similarly, in a separate U.N. policy statement issued on Nuclear Nonproliferation, Ban Ki-moon was quoted as stating *"[A]nd if our efforts also manage to address the social, economic, cultural and political conditions that aggravate terrorist attacks, so much the better."[3]*

Ultimately, the epiphany moment, where (according to *RedState. com*) everything "makes sense, a lot of sense," is when one realizes that, alternatively, *President Obama's political agenda has always dove-tailed and been consistently 100% in lockstep with the Multinational worldview of the United Nations – as opposed to what is in the best National Security interest as expressed by a clear majority of the American People.* Note that Rudy Giuliani was roundly criticized for inarticulately accusing Obama of not loving America enough. Well, we all love our country, including President Obama – but to varying degrees. Instead, with targeted specificity, Giuliani should have emphasized that President Obama – by his own actions – continually demonstrates *an even greater fidelity* that, not coincidentally, mirrors and coincides with the aspirations and objectives of the United Nations – more than the political views of the vast majority of the American People on virtually all foreign policy issues. There really is no other explanation or mystery here.

How Barack Obama's foreign policy decisions – throughout his Presidency – also telegraphed his ambition and intention to one day become the Secretary-General of the United Nations:

Both critics and Obama acolytes would dismiss the idea of Barack Obama one day becoming the Secretary-General of the United Nations as a "non-starter" given that either Russia and/or China would most assuredly exercise their U.N. Security Council Permanent Member veto power to his selection. Yet, why would Russian President Putin and/or China have anything to fear from Barack Obama as the Secretary-General of the United Nations "especially when one considers the added factor that, as President of the United States, Barack Obama has hardly played 'hard ball' or even 'laid a glove' on either Superpower?"[4] Illustratively, after Russia invaded the Ukraine in 2014, Barack Obama – who as President of the United States commands the mightiest military in the world – has been totally ineffectual ever since in convincing Putin to withdraw. Consequently, as Secretary-General of the United Nations, Barack Obama - without any military backing at all - would command even less respect from or powers of persuasion over Vladimir Putin, who would, thus have even less to fear from an Obama candidacy as U.N. Secretary-General.

Indeed, by his actions alone, a definitive and affirmative case can be made that what Barack Obama has really accomplished to a greater extent is more likely to have (consciously or unconsciously) curried favor with both Russia and China, but ultimately at the expense of failing to optimally advance and protect the National Security interests of the United States first and foremost. To that point, specifically, consider the following:

President Obama's considered signature foreign policy "achievement" during the first term of his Presidency is his 2011 nuclear weapons "reduction" agreement (many of his critics would say "unilateral agreement") that, according to *The Heritage Foundation*, in fact now A) still allows Russia to potentially "increase," rather than decrease, its nuclear warheads from 1,550 back to 2,200 and B) for the first time, permits Russia to launch ICBMs from mobile aircraft rather than only from previously identified (i.e. known) land-based stationary sites.[5]

Additionally:

1. Moreover, since 2014, it has only gotten worse - with Putin unilaterally annexing Crimea, and effectively, eastern Ukraine as well, with little pushback from the United States (beyond inconsequential economic sanctions). And now fully engaged in Syria.

2. While, in 2013, dubiously "sucking up" to China with a separate unilateral "giveaway agreement," which effectively shields China; requiring nothing of China to compel them to act on carbon pollution constraints before 2029 – but binds the United States to comply immediately.

3. The final piece integral to Barack Obama rounding out his U.N. Secretary-General Resume"[6] is the Iran Nuclear Deal that – instead of preventing Iran from obtaining a nuclear weapon – in essence, legally sanctions Iran as a nuclear weapons power no later than 2025 (unless Iran cheats and

surreptitiously builds one before then anyway; as clearly most of the American People believe).

Finally, when contrasted against being the President of the United States, as the Secretary-General of the United Nations, the United Nations would, indeed, be a perfect fit and, thus, probably appeal even more to Barack Obama than being President of the United States. Indeed, there would be no need to really govern anything; no opposition – essentially making pronouncements before like-minded disciples. Not unlike lecturing captive college class students or pontificating in the university academic faculty lounge at the University of Chicago Law School.

The investigation herein will continue to identify and analyze the foreign policy positions and decisions that Barack Obama and his Administration have taken during the now five years since the original publication of *Barack Obama's "Ultimate End Game"* in 2011. As a prerequisite and for continuity (to bring the reader "up to speed"), the chapter of this book to immediately follow is a summation of Chapter 18 of that 2011 book. In particular, the chapter chronicles those twelve specific events and decisions that shaped the direction of Barack Obama's U.S. foreign policy during the first two years of his presidency – evidencing an almost exclusive bias towards a Multinational (co-equal nations) worldview philosophy, mirroring that of the United Nations, rather than, as President of the United States; one best-suited to advancing the best National Security interests of the United States and the views held by the vast majority of the American People.

The noteworthy distinction herein is that the subsequent chapters will then delve into those individual foreign policy events and decisions that have subsequently occurred during the years 2011 through 2015 – but, this time additionally reflecting upon a comparative analysis of statements by President Obama to those previous U.N. policy statements predominantly made by the current and former United Nations Secretaries-General (Ban Ki-moon and Kofi Annan, respectively) to determine:

1. Whether A) those subsequent years' foreign policy decisions continue to be consistent with Barack Obama's preference for a Multinational worldview philosophy and, thus, B) continue to reject, at every turn, American Exceptionalism,[7] which espouses the belief that the United States is just as pragmatically and benevolently capable (if not more so) to spearhead and proactively promote peace worldwide as is the United Nations (Or, as Hillary Clinton contends, an indispensable force for good);

2. Identify and analyze those events and decisions wherein President Obama's preference for adopting the United Nations Multinational geo-political model of global governance in conducting U.S. foreign policy (i.e. The Obama Doctrine of "Leading from Behind") have militated against the best National Security interests of the American People;

3. Specifically how foreign policy decisions made by Barack Obama and his Administration during the 2011-2015 period reflected a definitive continuing pattern that was consistent with (and assiduously avoiding offending) the interests of U.N. Muslim nation states, which Mr. Obama will absolutely need to secure to one day be elected as Secretary-General of the United Nations and

4. Additional instances that occurred during his presidency, wherein decisions made and actions taken by Barack Obama, as President, are further reflective of a behavior and personal ambition consistent with his leaving the door open to one day becoming the Secretary-General of the United Nations.

Morally, there is certainly nothing wrong (and many may consider it even noble) that President Barack Obama may, indeed, hold a desire and intention to one day be elected as Secretary-General of the United Nations.However, in terms of what is in the best National Security interest of the United States and the American People, there exists a stark degree of divergence between the competing geo-political philosophies of American Exceptionalism, which Barack Obama rejects, and his demonstrated preference for the Multinational worldview espoused by the United Nations. **Secondly, throughout his Presidency, by consciously de-emphasizing the prominence of the United States as the world's leading nation in geopolitical influence, Barack Obama's actions will have diminished (i.e. "taken down") the United States' future role in world affairs while, simultaneously elevating the United Nations and, correspondingly, the stature and influence of its next Secretary-General in particular.**

However, if President Obama 1) fully intended to conduct U.S. foreign policy adhering exclusively to United Nations dogma and 2) held any desire to become the next U.N. Secretary-General after leaving the White House in 2017, he cannot escape that he had a moral obligation to have disclosed to the American People his intent and ambition precisely because the voting electorate had the right to know it from the beginning. It would then have rightly been within the purview of the American electorate – in both the 2008 and 2012 Presidential Elections - to have determined to what degree the motivational and U.S. foreign policy decision-making process of Barack Obama, as President of the United States, had conflicted with or been driven by any quest by him to, one day, become the United Nations Secretary-General.

The Vatican and United Nations Analogy

Moreover, a parallel and revealing analogy can be drawn from the Presidential Election of 1960 to the moral question as to Barack Obama, as President of the United States, elevating and implementing the Multinational worldview of the United Nations above and at the expense of the optimal National Security best interests of the American People. Specifically, during the 1960 Presidential Campaign, the concern was raised by many as to whether Senator John F. Kennedy, as President of the United States, would allow himself to be influenced by the Pope in either foreign or domestic policy – thus elevating his primary allegiance to the Vatican (i.e. a world body and international organization) and his Catholic religion above that, and "at the expense" of the American People.

In fact, during the course of the campaign, this concern had reach such a crescendo that then-Senator Kennedy felt politically compelled to confront it head-on to reassure the American People *before the Presidential Election*; in a major address appearing before the predominantly Protestant Greater Houston Ministerial Association in September 1960. In particular, Kennedy felt it necessary to reassure non-Catholics of his belief that his allegiance, as President of United States, would, at all times, require him to serve the best interests of the American People first and foremost. **Thus, John F. Kennedy believed that, under no circumstance should a President of the United States morally or legally allow him or**

herself to be guided or influenced in any way by any global body or international organization – or as in his particular case – the Vatican.

Furthermore, although Kennedy was motivated politically to confront this issue head on, he had no moral or legal obligation to do so *unless* he, in fact, did intend to elevate the dictates and views of the Vatican above his paramount legal responsibility as President of the United States to serve the best interests of the American People – which, of course, he did not.

No one was questioning Kennedy's patriotism as an American – nor should anyone herein question President Obama's patriotism either. Regardless as to whether Barack Obama wants to one day become the Secretary-General of the United Nations after leaving office in 2017 or not.

However, applying the analogy drawn herein to President Kennedy and the Vatican, if Barack Obama fully intended from the outset of his Presidency to allow himself to A) be significantly influenced by the United Nations (i.e. a global body and international organization) and adopt its Multinational worldview philosophy in executing United States foreign policy and B) have held an ambition in becoming the next Secretary-General of the United Nations after leaving office, Mr. Obama had, at a minimum, a moral obligation to have informed the American People of his intentions from the outset.

And if so, having therefore consciously chosen *not* to inform the American People of his true intentions, from the outset, is at least as much a moral failure as President Obama and his Administration having lied to the American People about Obamacare – for which opinion polls subsequently revealed that, if known, Barack Obama would have, otherwise, lost the 2012 Presidential Election:

> The most grievous consequence to the country was that President Obama (not unlike Richard Nixon in 1972) was also consciously willing, at all costs, to mislead (i.e. "lie") and subvert the Presidential Election process in 2012 ("The Means") just to insure preventing the demise of ObamaCare - which most assuredly would have followed had he not been re-elected. And, as evidence, one need only look to polls taken - one year later – after, according to *Politifact*, Barack Obama's "Lie of the Year" was exposed ("If you want to keep your Health Care plan – you can keep it"). To wit, had the President been truthful about ObamaCare, based on a representative number of Obama Voters who would have otherwise changed their ballot and voted against him in 2012, Barack Obama would, indeed, have lost the popular vote (i.e. Three opinion polls: 1) ABC/Washington Post – November 2013; 2) Wilson Perkins Allen Opinion Research – November 2013 and 3) The Economist – February 2014).[8]

Moreover, regarding a potential legal obligation, based on the comparative analysis performed herein of United Nations policy statements and speeches, President Obama appeared to have advanced and elevated United Nations policies and objectives above and to the detriment of the best National Security and domestic interests of the American People specifically pertaining to at least the following five policy matters:

1. **U.S. Border Security and Illegal Immigration Enforcement:** Throughout his Presidency, Barack Obama has purposely and repeatedly A) ignored materially

strengthening U.S. Border Security and B) failed to prioritize the overhaul of an inadequate and lax deportation system to drastically expedite the immigrant deportation judicial process of convicted criminals in accordance with United Nations Immigration doctrine. In particular, nearly 200,000 criminal aliens have been paroled under the Obama Administration while awaiting U.S. immigration deportation hearings and, in the meantime, were allowed to legally walk the streets of America. However, note that in 2013 alone, more than 1,000 illegal immigrants with criminal records who were released by Immigration and Customs Enforcement (ICE) to await deportation hearings – within one year's time – had gone on to commit new hardcore felony offenses (Chapter 5).

2. **Closing GTMO:** Given that the United Nations has steadfastly called for the closing of the Guantanamo Bay terrorist prison facility since 2006, considering it a violation of international human law, President Obama remains determined to close GTMO by accelerating the release of terrorist detainees – many of whom had heretofore been determined to be a threat to return to the War on Terror. Thus they remain a National Security Threat to this country and the American People (Chapter 6)

3. **The Iran Nuclear Deal:** Barack Obama himself (and evidently in concert with the United Nations) is effectively granting Iran the legal right to permanently obtain nuclear weapons within the next 10-15 years in violation of the specific tenets of the Nuclear Non-Proliferation Treaty (Chapter 8).

4. **The War against ISIS:** President Obama has refused to ramp up U.S. military attacks and to commit the requisite

level of U.S. troops necessary to defeat ISIS – inhibited in no small part by his hyper-concern about incurring potential "war crimes" accusations and charges from the United Nations concerning unintentionally excessive civilian collateral casualties resulting from any future military strikes (Chapter 7). Moreover, now in the wake of the October 2015 "friendly fire" U.S. attack on the Doctors Without Borders hospital that killed 22 in Kunduz, Afghanistan, it is even harder to imagine that Barack Obama will be authorizing any expansion of military strikes against ISIS in Iraq throughout the remainder of his Presidency and

5. **Climate Change:** The Obama Administration has imposed upon the American People excessive and exceedingly costly governmental regulation at the expense of and stunting the recovery and growth of the U.S. economy - driven by an Environmental policy that mirrors the hyper-concern of the United Nations' Number One priority i.e. the so-called imminent and substantial threat posed by Climate Change (Chapter 3).

"On all these issues, but particularly missile defense [i.e. a hoped-for second further nuclear disarmament reduction agreement], this can be solved, but it is important for him [Vladimir Putin] to give me space. This is my last Election. After my [2012] Election, I will have more flexibility."
President Barack Obama March 26, 2012 (Unbeknownst - before an open microphone confiding to then-"puppet" Russian Prime Minister Dmitri Medvedev)

Yet, one wonders how it is that Barack Obama, as President of the United States, could rationalize confiding in Russian Dictator Vladimir Putin (through Medvedev) concerning the utmost matters of U.S. National Security (i.e. nuclear weapons) that which he clearly had no intention of disclosing to the American people - certainly before the 2012 Presidential Election? But if President Obama truly felt at that moment in time that – in accordance with his sworn oath – he was acting in the best National Security interests of the American People, why was he so concerned about concealing from the American People his desire for a further reduction in the nuclear arsenal of the United States until after the 2012 Presidential Election? Evidently, Vladimir Putin can be privy to matters affecting U.S. National Security that the American People cannot and somehow one is still to conclude that President Obama is acting in the best National Security interest of the American People.

Could this have possibly been the one and only documented instance throughout his Presidency where Barack Obama – elevating his own political legacy ambitions above the interests of the American people - felt it necessary and/or expedient to purposely conceal his true intentions and beliefs from the American People? Not hardly. As previously mentioned, recall the lies of the Obama Administration and President Obama himself – admitted to in 2013 – concerning Obamacare that secured its continuance and got him past the 2012 Presidential Election.

The Day Barack Obama's Dream of Becoming the Next U.N. Secretary-General in 2017 Ended

Of course, in retrospect, any designs Barack Obama had of becoming the next Secretary-General of the United Nations after leaving office in January 2017 ultimately began to unravel, in the sixth year of his Presidency, when on March 18, 2014 Russian President Vladimir Putin officially annexed the Ukrainian Territory of Crimea. Subsequently in November 2014, Putin covertly expanded his incursion into the eastern provinces of Ukraine bordering on Russia with both troops and material – and has maintained that ongoing occupation there to this very day.

> **Rumors are floating back from the Middle East that [Barack Obama] is sounding out Democrats, Republicans and friends of the United Nations in the United States to help get the job of Secretary-General of the U.N.**
> *The Washington Times* "A New Job for the President – His Friends Think He's a Natural for the U.N." –January 12, 2016

Nevertheless as late as January 2016, it was reported that Barack Obama apparently made one last gasp "behind-the-scenes" effort at a run for the job of United Nations Secretary-General. However, there would still be no hoped-for political reconciliation between Barack Obama and Vladimir Putin, whose approval was essential to any desire Obama still held of becoming the next U.N. Secretary-General in 2017.

Ultimately in October 2016, Antonio Guterres was elected to succeed Ban Ki-moon as the next Secretary-General of the United Nations. Although, even if Barack Obama now has to wait two terms (i.e. currently ten years) to succeed Guterres in 2027, 1) he would still only be 65-years old and 2) his resume would no doubt still be formidable, based upon his devotion and unflinching commitment to the principles of Global Governance and "co-equal nations," as demonstrated in his conduct of all facets of U.S. foreign policy throughout his eight years as President of the United States.

CHAPTER 1

1 Original Source Reference: Chapter 18; page 263 – *Barack Obama's "Ultimate End Game"* by Gary Patterson (Copyright 2011).

2 *CNN Politics* "U.N. Security Council Unanimously Passes Anti-Terrorism Resolution" by Greg Botelho, Jim Acosta and Elizabeth Hartfield – September 24, 2014.

3 *UN Office For Disarmament Affairs* "The United Nations and Security in a Nuclear World-The Secretary-General's Five-Point Plan Proposal on Nuclear Disarmament" (Copyright 2015).

4 *Barack Obama's "Ultimate End Game"* - Ibid - Page 285.

5 Source: *The Heritage Foundation* "An Independent Assessment of New START" –April 30, 2010.

6 Which Obama literally began working towards on "Day One" of his presidency (i.e. Vowing to close Gitmo).

7 The classic interpretation of American Exceptionalism extols the virtues and uniqueness of this nation referring to "the special character of the United States as a uniquely free nation based on democratic ideals and personal liberty." - Ian Tyrrell – "What is American exceptionalism?" – wordpress.com/papers.

8 *America at the Precipice – **Restoring** the Plummeting Middle Class Standard of Living* by Gary R. Patterson (Copyright 2014) Pages 5-6.

OBAMA PRO-UNITED NATIONS
"MULTINATIONAL WORLDVIEW" DECISIONS
(W.W.U.N.D.? - What Would the United Nations Do?)

1. Obama vows to close Gitmo within one year - decrying negative image of America throughout the world. (January 2009)

2. Obama admonishes America as being "arrogant and dismissive." (April 2009)

3. Obama's Worldwide "American Apology Tour" begins in Cairo. (June 2009)

4. In opposition to the accepted description of America as built on a Judeo-Christian ethic, Obama proclaims that the United States is neither a Christian, Jewish or Muslim nation. (June 2009)

5. Obama refuses to overrule Attorney General Eric Holder's decision to hold 911 *civilian trials* in New York City (September 2009)

6. In his first United Nations speech, Obama chooses to criticize Israel. (September 2009)

7. However, Obama chooses not to confront Iran at the United Nations with the discovery of construction of a secret uranium enrichment facility as a prelude and a prerequisite to developing a nuclear weapon. (September 2009)

8. President Obama wouldn't go to Berlin, thus, downplaying the significance of the celebration of the 20th anniversary of the Cold War victory of the United States and Europe over the Soviet Union. (November 2009) Yet, in 2008, Obama enthusiastically showed up in Berlin knowing that he personally would be lauded for his Multinational (co-equal-nations) worldview agenda - rejecting American Exceptionalism.

9. Obama initially downplays the possibility that the Ft. Hood Mass Murderer had terrorist connections. (November 2009)

10. Obama initially downplays the possibility that the "Underwear Bomber" had terrorist connections. (December 2009)

11. NASA Director discloses that, according to President Obama, his primary directive is to reach out and extol Muslim contributions to science (huh?). (July 2010)

12. Obama voices support for the construction of the Ground Zero Mosque in lower Manhattan. (August 2010).

Barack Obama's "Ultimate End Game": The United Nations - Part I (2009 – 2010)[9]

> *"It's inexplicable why he [President Obama] did this. He went out of his way to do this…It's ridiculous. It's absurd. I'm baffled. I'm astonished."*
> Dick Morris – Conservative Pollster and Political Commentator - *Fox News -The O'Reilly Factor* – August 18, 2010

> *"It's almost self-destructive."*
> Bill O'Reilly – Political Commentator - *Fox News - The O'Reilly Factor* – August 18, 2010

In the aftermath of President Obama's initial pronouncement of support for the constitutional right of Imam Feisal Abdul Rauf to build the so-called Ground Zero Mosque (August 13, 2010), Bill O'Reilly and Dick Morris were commiserating as to why, from purely a political perspective, would Barack Obama voluntarily choose to weigh in, at all, declaring his open support for the Mosque's construction:

> **"Let me be clear: as a citizen, and as President, I believe Muslims have the same right to practice religion in this**

> *country. That includes the right to build a place of wor-*
> *ship and a community center on private property in lower*
> *Manhattan."*
> President Barack Obama - Ramadan If tar White House
> Dinner – August 13, 2010

Although, the morning following his speech, President Obama felt it necessary to pro-actively seek out the press and disclaim ("walk back") any implication of his own *personal desire* to see the Mosque's construction - to the consternation and wonderment of virtually everyone on either side of the issue. What is most significant, Morris rightly noted that, until that speech, President Obama, through his then-Press Secretary Robert Gibbs, had declared the controversy surrounding the Ground Zero Mosque to be "a local issue" - taking the politically correct and expedient "hands-off" approach.

Both O'Reilly and Morris - and virtually all other political pundits of both the Left and Right - agreed that, politically, there was absolutely no upside for President Obama to have - of his own volition - chosen to inject himself at the focal point of this dispute. Consequently, the question remained: Why then did he feel compelled to do so? What was his motivation?

However, the conclusions drawn, not only by Morris and O'Reilly, but by virtually all pundits of all political persuasions, are based on an engrained and presumed belief and paradigm that, the ultimate political "End Game" of any President of the United States (or anyone with aspirations to be President) is to be re-elected to a second term - connoting a successful presidency from a presidential legacy perspective.

But, what if, after serving out a two-term Presidency, Barack

Obama doesn't intend to retire, but has further political ambitions to then become Secretary-General of the United Nations, as well, after leaving the White House? What if that is Barack Obama's "Ultimate End Game?" Indeed, note that, not just one or two or six - but all of President Obama's twelve U.N. worldview-like responses to the events listed at the beginning of this Chapter would have passed muster with the overwhelming support of the United Nations General Assembly of States and, especially, Muslim nation member states.

And the purpose of the discussion here makes no value judgment as to whether going on to be a United Nations Secretary-General is a good or bad ambition for President Obama - or anyone - to have. Nor can anyone except President Obama know whether his motivation is one driven by true altruism or as a political legacy enhancement - or to some degree both. And, for someone who is described by many as more of a "Grand Designs" – rather than a "Details" kinda guy best known as a charismatic and inspirational orator, it is understandable how being the United Nations Secretary-General would appeal to Barack Obama (perhaps even more than being President of the United States).

However, if President Obama does hold an ambition to also, one day, become the next United Nations Secretary-General, the American People have the right to know it. Not only whether they may care or not but - more significantly - to determine for themselves what degree is the motivational and decision-making process of Barack Obama, as President of the United States, colored, driven or influenced by any future desire to, one day, become the next United Nations Secretary-General.

Additionally, it is intriguing to contemplate that, if President

Obama holds such an ambition to - one day - "run for" or be named the Secretary-General of the United Nations after leaving the White House, all of the twelve issues and related stances taken by President Obama since becoming President of the United States (listed at the beginning of this Chapter), would explain, be consistent with and serve to enhance a future United Nations Secretary-General candidacy. Moreover, even the two books written by Obama, about himself, before becoming President, consciously accentuated certainly more of a preference for the United Nations-"Multinational" worldview philosophy among nations than one promoting the merely "parochial virtues" emphasizing American Exceptionalism and Individualism first. Could this also be consistent with, and at the root of President Obama's actual demonstrative initial reluctance to wearing an American flag lapel pin as well?

Moreover, a review of every issue and position taken (per the list appearing at the beginning of the Chapter) is consistent with and considered favorable by the current worldview consensus of a majority of United Nations Muslim member nations; whose endorsement would also be considered crucial to any future candidacy by Barack Obama to become the United Nations Secretary-General one day. And, without the support of the U.N. Muslim nation states, the hope of any former American President ever becoming United Nations Secretary-General would, indeed, be a non-starter. However, unless purely coincidental, every position taken by President Obama, per this list, is also in virtual lockstep with respect to the Muslim world consensus view - as if consciously crafted by President Obama to pave the way towards leaving that door open one day.

September 2009 – Obama's Image Debut at the U.N. as a Non-Confrontational World Peacemaker

President Obama 'kicked it off" with his pro-active "world apology tour" in Cairo in June 2009, for what he termed as America's mistakes and hegemony over the decades – rejecting any reference to American Exceptionalism. Even more curious - yet consistent with the motivation of Barack Obama in downplaying confrontation as a demonstration of his peace-making prowess - is what occurred in September of 2009 when President Obama had his first opportunity to preside at the United Nations, as Chair of the Security Council session on Nuclear Non-Proliferation - Obama's stated signature world achievement goal.

In particular, just days earlier, unbeknownst to Iran, the United States and its European allies France and Germany, had confirmed proof that Iran had been developing a secret weapons-grade uranium enrichment facility - in naked violation of the Nuclear Non-Proliferation Treaty of which Iran is a signatory. For maximum impact at the United Nations and worldwide, both French President Nicolas Sarkozy and German Prime Minister Andrea Merkel believed and urged that President Obama confront Iran with this discovery during the Security Council Meeting. However, Sarkozy and Merkel were rebuff and overruled - being told by Obama Administration officials "that, to do so on that occasion, would have overshadowed and potentially spoiled 'the image of success for Mr. Obama's debut at the United Nations...'".[10]

To the contrary, to have confronted Iran - unawares - at the United Nations Security Council Meeting "would have been reminiscent and rivaled Adlai Stevenson's dramatic confrontation of the Soviet ambassador at the United Nations at the height of the 1962 Cuban Missile Crisis ("I'm prepared to wait until hell freezes over for your response.")...Further, even if the overriding concern of the Obama Administration "spin doctors" was what's best for President Obama's political image on a world stage, wouldn't the dramatic and momentous impact of this disclosure - live; at the United Nations during a Security Council session (incidentally) on Nuclear Non-Proliferation - have, collaterally, accomplished their misguided political image priority anyway?"[11] But, maybe not if, in their estimation, paving the way for a future run at being the next United Nations Secretary-General - by showing Obama as "non-confrontational" - was considered to be of greater import than deterring Iran's unchecked and undeterred advance towards gaining a nuclear weapon.

Again, in the context of this discussion, no value judgment is being drawn here should President Obama truly be desirous of, one day, becoming the United Nations Secretary-General. And if much of President Obama's "worldview" (at least with respect to those twelve incidents and issues listed at the beginning of this Chapter) happens to coincide with the consensus views of the Third World nations that have held sway in the United Nations over the past 40 years, he need not apologize or change them.

However, reiterating: the American People have the right to know if President Obama holds an ambition to, one day, become United Nations Secretary-General. And, if so, then the American people can decide for themselves as to whether they are concerned or not as to what degree Barack Obama's attitudes and judgment - regarding U.S. foreign policy issues - may or may not conflict with U.S. National Security, domestic security and consequently, the best interest of the American People. Namely, whether Barack Obama's decisions as President of the United States may or may not be influenced, tempered or constricted by any such future world ambition to segue into becoming the next

Secretary-General of the United Nations after leaving the White House in 2017.

July 2008 - Obama's Berlin Debut

Candidate Barack Obama and his presidential campaign handlers enthusiastically strode into Berlin, in July 2008, with the spotlight clearly on him. President Obama would use that inaugural moment, on the world stage, as an opportunity to ingratiate himself with the United Nations and its leaders by declaring to the world that day his Multinational view of co-equal nations - rejecting any vestige of American Exceptionalism.

However, when invited one year later in November 2009, as the President of the United States, by German Prime Minister Merkel to attend the 20th Anniversary of the Fall of the Berlin Wall as the prelude to the End of the Cold War - the epic 45-year head-to-head struggle of our time against Communism during the last half of the 20th Century - President Obama declined; his aides citing "scheduling conflicts."

Although, was the President's reticence to attend and highlight this momentous occasion driven more by a conscious effort, on his part, to downplay the predominant role of the United States, as the remaining world superpower, in defeating Soviet Communism? Did President Obama see his presence, in Berlin, celebrating such an occasion as 1) being contrary to and at cross purposes with his personal embracement of a Multinational co-equal nations philosophy and therefore 2) displeasing to the United Nations, given its penchant for Global Governance?

President Obama's Re-Election Probability In 2012 - A Cautionary Tale for the GOP

(Again, note that Part I (2009-2010) was originally written and published in March 2011 – 18 months <u>before</u> the 2012 Presidential Election)

> *"Why would you do that? Why would you put yourself on the opposite side of issues where 70% of Americans disagree with you?"*
> Newt Gingrich - *Fox News -On The Record* – September 17, 2010

From a political perspective, Gingrich too (like Dick Morris and Bill O'Reilly) could not understand why President Obama would choose such unpopular stances on major political issues and incidents that would clearly put him at odds with a decided majority of the American People. But even pragmatic Democrat politicians and pundits as well must have cringed at many of the stances President Obama voluntarily chose to take (concerning the list of twelve incidents and issues appearing at the beginning of this Chapter) approaching the 2010 Mid-Term Elections. And, if re-election in 2012 was a paramount political legacy consideration - or, at a minimum, a necessary predicate act - to becoming the next United Nations Secretary-General one day, President Obama might wish to consider "walking back" or somehow tempering his positions on at least some of these twelve events and issues before the 2012 Presidential Election.

Indeed, opponents may raise the issue that the positions taken by President Obama (per the list) combined with the overall current malaise of the American economy and the Obama Presidency thus far (in 2010) could reasonably be expected to culminate in his defeat for re-election in 2012 (or, as O'Reilly mused, may be "almost self-destructive").

However, to the contrary:

1) **It is both the Republican Party and Conservatives who would be wise not to underestimate President Obama's re-election possibilities - even in light of the considered less-than-successful first 18 months of his Presidency (through July 2010).** Aside from a Media that likely will still be overwhelmingly "in the tank" for Obama, consider that, in 2012, so long as Obama can again count on 95% of the black vote and 80% of the Hispanic vote (due in large part to President Obama's continued conscious demagoguing of the Immigration issue),[12] the Democrats would need only 42% of the remaining Voter electorate to achieve just 50%+ of the popular vote.[13] Conversely stated, the GOP would need a landslide-like 58% of the remaining Voter electorate (a formidable task) to achieve just 50%+ of the popular vote nationwide.[14]

More specifically, given that most all demographic group Voter patterns typically fall along traditional lines, the only significant dynamic Voter demographic "swing" group that "is still up for grabs" - and generally determines presidential elections - is White Independent Voters.[15] However, assuming the anticipated overwhelming support for Obama among Black and Hispanic Voters in 2012 as described herein, Republicans would still need to win a landslide-like 62% of the White Independent Vote to attain just 50%+ of the popular vote in 2012.

2) Further, Republicans should not be lulled into a false sense of security by the landslide Democrat "shellacking" in the 2010 Mid-Term Congressional Elections. With David Plouffe at the helm again of the Obama "Get-Out-The-Vote" drive in 2012, given his meteoric success in 2008, the Democrats will again, indeed, get the vote out

in 2012. And Plouffe will bring at least the same, if not more fervor and refinement of his Democrat Voter Recruitment expertise in 2012.

In particular, the key element to the Democrats' success in 2012 will be - as in 2008 - getting that subset of their Democrat constituencies to the polls that would not, otherwise, typically show up on their own. Further, demographically, many of these targeted Democrat constituent Voters either pay no income tax and/or are the one out of six Americans who are dependent on the Federal government for financial assistance.

No doubt, Plouffe will find every one of them again in 2012 and see to it that every targeted Democrat Voter will get multiple robo-calls throughout the Election period. Moreover, on Election Day 2012 (or throughout the Voting period), in every "battleground state," Democrat Precinct Wardens will have their legion of drivers "at the ready" to make certain that these Voters get to the polls - whether they have a phone or not. And, although you will never hear it said in a robo-call (which could be made public), rest assured that those Democrat precinct drivers will get their point across to these targeted Democrat Voters - on the way to the polls - that a Republican President could or would, if elected, take their government assistance away. Rest assured that it will be stated that bluntly.

And one should not be so naïve as to think that the Democrats, under Plouffe's command, are going to allow themselves to lose the 2012 Presidential Election for want of not having enough precinct Election drivers. They will even have performed "dry runs" in the days leading up to the Election to insure that they know exactly where these targeted Voters can be found.

Further, much was made of the "shellacking" that President Obama and the Democrats took in the 2010 Mid-Term Elections - having been soundly beaten 55% to 45% by the Republicans, or 41 million votes to 34 million; resulting in a 7 million Vote edge for the GOP. Sounds good.

However, ABC News Pollster Gary Langer projected that a net additional 10 million more 2008 Obama Voters (than 2008 McCain Voters) didn't even show up for the 2010 Mid-Term Elections.[16] Further, assume that these additional 10 million Obama Voter "no shows" had, indeed, voted and – like "late-deciding" Voters – had voted 80% for Democrats. Rather than a 7 million Voter edge, the Republican Voter edge would have been reduced to a relatively miniscule one million votes; or, from a 10 percentage-point edge (55% to 45%) to 1% of the total Mid-Term vote. The Lesson: Reiterating, Plouffe will find all of these 2010 Obama Voter "no shows" in 2012. Count on it.

3) Additionally, most pundits can't imagine the nadir of President Obama's Presidency being any lower than it already was in 2010. However, even so, the President still managed to maintain a Presidential Job Approval Rating in the 40-45 percent range. Similarly, it should be noted that, consistent with that low-to-mid-forties Presidential Job Approval, the number of Americans who currently pay no income tax and/or receive government financial assistance (and for the most part then feel beholden and typically vote Democrat) is roughly that same 45% figure. As a consequence, if as polls indicate, it is unlikely that President Obama's Job Approval Rating will ever go below 40%; that is still a formidable springboard from which to launch a re-election bid. **To wit, President Obama would only need to convince an additional 5-10% of the remaining 55% of the Voting electorate, going into the 2012 Election,**

that he is doing, at least, an adequate or acceptable job and show up to vote for him.

Further, even in light of their 2010 Mid-Term elections drubbing, President Obama and the Democrats still retained a 2 to 1 Voter support advantage among Unmarried Woman Voters – a highly pivotal demographic group that, in 2008, represented 21% (or 1 in 5) of all Voters – which could prove particularly ominous again for the GOP in 2012. Similarly, and just as portentous, Young Voters (i.e. age 18 to 29), who also represented 1 in 5 Voters in 2008, again voted decidedly Democrat in the 2010 Mid-Terms. The difference in 2010: Only half of them decided - on their own - to show up. Plouffe will see to it that won't be the case in 2012.

4) In rebuttal, Obama acolytes will point to the politically unpopular positions taken by the President and the Obama Administration in A) the challenge to the Arizona Immigration Law; B) the Professor Gates/Cambridge, MA police incident[17] and C) the declination to prosecute in the Black Panther Voter Intimidation case in Philadelphia, as further evidence that President Obama is a man of principal and not influenced by opinion polls. Yet - politically - the very positions taken by the Obama Administration, in each of these cases, suggests a more likely political ulterior motive by the President meant to solidify and galvanize his support among Hispanic and Black Voters going into the 2012 Presidential Election. As Rahm Emmanuel might say: Never waste taking advantage of a crisis opportunity to galvanize, reconstitute and reinvigorate your core Voter demographic constituent groups to get to the polls.

5) Moreover, the Republicans will not only have to overcome just a 7% margin of victory as occurred in 2008 - but rather an 11% Democrat margin of victory. Specifically, an even more critical

swing factor in favor of the Democrats, this time, in 2012 will be those disgruntled Hillary Clinton Supporters – that amounted to 2% of all Voters - who voted against Obama and for McCain in 2008. In particular, had those disgruntled Hillary Supporters voted for Obama instead of McCain, Obama's 7% winning margin (53% to 46%) would, in actuality, have been more of a landslide-like 11% over the GOP in 2008.

It is reasonable to assume that those Hillary Supporters will, this time, vote for Obama in 2012 (especially if Obama has the foresight to name Clinton to his 2012 Democrat ticket as his Vice-President). Moreover, why wouldn't the Democrats do, at least, as well or better in 2012 – especially if, this time, Hillary Clinton were on the ticket, against a GOP ticket that, most likely, will again be two White guys.

Republicans may take comfort in the 2010 Mid-Term elections, noting that the GOP won the overall Female Vote - 49% to 48% for the first time in decades. Yet, a 1% GOP edge in the Female Vote in 2010 is a false sense of security when one considers that the Voter demographics in a Mid-Term election are always more Whiter and older (i.e. GOP-dominated) than in a Presidential Election. **Finally, it needs to be remembered that the Republican Party has only won the popular vote once in the last five Presidential Elections.**

ﮊﮊﮊ

Obama's Actual Chance of Becoming U.N. Secretary-General

Although it would not occur to most Americans - or political pundits for that matter - that a U.S. President might have any political ambition beyond a two-term presidency, if it were possible, conceivably someone, like former President Bill Clinton would likely have jumped at the chance to be Secretary-General of the United

Nations. Many Americans might not consider such an appointment as a legacy enhancement and, perhaps, just the opposite - given the low opinion that most Conservatives hold for the accomplishments (or lack thereof) and political direction that the United Nations has taken over the last 40 years. However, it is not necessary that one agree with such an ambition for it to be plausible and compelling for another.

But, President Obama is entitled to his own paradigm and, with the possibility of a Democrat following him into the White House in 2017,[18] the influence and sway that he may perceive he could wield as the United Nations Secretary-General may appear quite appealing and even compelling to him. Indeed, one cannot deny that the foreign policy positions and decisions that President Obama has taken on each of the twelve issues (listed at the beginning of this Chapter) are identically compatible with those of the third world nations of the U.N. - not the least of which, the Muslim nations that Obama must persuade should he ever want to become the United Nations Secretary-General one day.

And, although the Ultra-Leftist likes of George Soros and the Daily Kos might applaud a United Nations agenda that, among other things, endorses a worldwide Carbon Tax (that even the United Nations committee co-chair on Climate Change freely admits will serve to promote international "wealth redistribution" – Sound Familiar?), most of Middle America considers such an idea as prohibitively costly and, thus, an anathema to the best National Interests of the American People.

Ultimately, somebody from the media needs to ask President Obama. Of course, with a glib smile and smug laugh, President Obama would attempt to dismiss such a suggestion, out of hand, noting that citizens of the permanent member states of the United Nations Security Council (like the U.S.) are not eligible to be elected U.N. Secretary-General. End of discussion (he hopes). The original rationale behind this informal rule being that the United Nations did not want to "invest an unwise amount of leverage over international decisions in one government, notwithstanding the statutory independence of the office." [19] Nevertheless, this U.N. stipulation, although considered traditional, is only an "informal rule" and not specifically prohibited by the United Nations Charter.

Anticipated Criticism and Rebuttal

Further, supporters might point to President Obama's decision to escalate drone attacks against Al Qaeda in Pakistan (in 2009-2010) as contrary evidence of an instance where the United Nations might consider such military action in a negative light towards the United States and President Obama in particular. However, in this singular instance, President Obama had no choice in that, throughout the 2008 campaign, he argued politically and persistently for the need to prevail in Afghanistan. For him to have curtailed drone attacks against Al Qaeda in Pakistan was not an option.

Specifically, in the event of a future attack on American soil, President Obama would have left himself vulnerable and, likely, would never have recovered politically had he previously elected to back off or curtail the drone attacks in Pakistan. His political career, including any thought of a second Presidential term and to one day become United Nations Secretary-General would be dead in the water.

Although, one must remember that it was Barack Obama himself, in 2007-2008, who chose to paint himself into this corner by supporting the Afghan War as 'the good war" - attempting to advance the clear implication in the minds of Voters that United States' involvement in the Iraq War was not. Secondly, many believe that, in 2008, Obama's overt support for winning the Afghan War served the dual purpose of demonstrating an aggressive stance on foreign policy matters - blunting criticism, at the time, from the Clinton campaign challenge.

However, regardless of potential United Nations member state criticism, on this one foreign policy issue, there was no turning back. There was no other choice to make. The stakes were too high. Consequently, maintaining and - to his credit – intensifying those drone attacks, during his first term, against Al Qaeda in Pakistan would serve as President Obama's domestic "political firewall" against criticism should there ever be another devastating attack by Al Qaeda on American soil. Alternatively, given his perceived aggressive stance against Al Qaeda in Pakistan, if, regrettably, such an attack did occur on American soil, politically, support for President Obama would most likely soar - as it did for President Bush in 2002, the year following 9/11.

Obama's Semantic Distinctions Regarding the War on Terror

But, even then, only in his own mind, could President Obama perceive that he could somehow "soften the blow" by attempting to draw a meaningful distinction in recasting the Global War on Terror as something less than that. To wit, presumably, in an effort to de-emphasize the War against Al Qaeda and curry favor with or assuage the Muslim world, the Obama Administration 1) ordered The Department of Homeland Security to re-name it a "Man-Caused Disaster" (what does that mean?) and 2) The Pentagon to refer to it henceforth as an "Overseas Contingency Action."

Given his own admission of "being in a White House bubble" as President, Mr. Obama, indeed at times does appear to operate in a vacuum - lacking a perceptual frame of reference – erroneously believing, as in this instance, that this game of semantics would somehow cleverly convince someone other than himself.[20] In his mind, it might score decisive nuanced debating style points at Harvard, but, to the American People, it doesn't wash and, if anything, is no more than a distinction without a difference. Regrettably, the only thing actually accomplished by such a semantic exercise turns out to be a negative one. Namely, it only serves as a further impetus for our enemy, Al Qaeda, which interprets it as a further sign of weakness – displaying both a lack of nerve and resolve, as well as naiveté, on the part of President Obama.

Enthusiastic Support among U.N. General Assembly Nations

Finally, as to the question of support for Barack Obama among the U.N. General Assembly of nations, consider the following talk based on discussions during the 2008 U.S. Presidential Election with United Nations officials, who could only give their insight anonymously because of official U.N. policy that prohibits the expression of a political preference in U.S. Presidential Elections:

1. "Obama supporters (at the United Nations) hail from Russia, Canada, France, Britain, Germany, the Netherlands, Sierra Leone, South Africa, Indonesia and elsewhere...Many U.N. rank and file...see in Obama's multicultural background - a Kenyan father, an Indonesian stepfather and a mother and grandparents from Kansas - a reflection of themselves. 'We do not consider him an African American, said Congo's U.N. ambassador, Atoki Ileka, 'We consider him an African.'"

2. "The Obama (U.S. presidential) candidacy has enormous emotional resonance among delegates from developing countries...And Kofi Annan, the first black U.N. Secretary General, said the prospects of an Obama presidency would be 'phenomenal.'" [21]

Moreover, the list of twelve major U.S. foreign policy decisions made by President Obama thus far (at issue and highlighted for discussion in this Chapter) are, indeed, textbook responses that could be touted by Obama, one day, as being in total compliance with the United Nations' anti-superpower, Multinational world-view philosophy. Indeed, this list of "United Nations-Friendly" U.S. foreign policy decisions made by President Obama during the first two years of his Presidency, could serve as "Exhibit A" in support of a future effort by Mr. Obama to become the Secretary-General of the United Nations.

Russia and China Veto Power

Although, critics would also point to either Russia or China or both - having veto power as permanent members of the United Nations Security Council - who would surely exercise it at the thought of a former American President becoming U.N. Secretary-General. However, with each successive five-year election cycle of a U.N. Secretary-General, there has been increased support among member nations for a greater voice of the General Assembly of nations in the selection process and a call for more openness. Heretofore, the U.N. General Assembly has been restricted to only voting upon the limited number of candidates exclusively hand-picked by the Security Council. One current recommendation for the future selection process of U.N. Secretary-General proffered by some middle-power nation members, including India, specifically calls for "a stronger role for the General Assembly in proposing and vetting candidates under consideration."[22]

However, even if Russia and/or China would like to veto an Obama candidacy for U.N. Secretary-General, in light of this apparent robust, broad-based consensus of goodwill for Barack Obama that exists among the U.N. General Assembly member nations, would either Russia or China necessarily want to be seen as standing in the way? Moreover, what would China or Russia really have to fear from Obama as U.N. Secretary-General as evidenced during his first two years as President, in that Barack Obama has hardly held sway over either country. Specifically, concerning Russia, did Putin not get President Obama to concede the NATO Missile Defense System in Poland (in 2009) in exchange for absolutely nothing in return, in terms of cooperation, on Iran?

Although, there was a response from Russia and it was, ominously, not positive. Reportedly, Russia, in October 2010, entered into another agreement to build a nuclear power facility for another rogue oil-rich nation (like Iran) with no apparent peaceful energy need for it. This time it is Venezuela - in the Western Hemisphere - and its anti-American (then-) Dictator, Hugo Chavez. And regarding China, as long as it continues to hold the United States as a monetary hostage for the indefinite future in financing our double-digit Trillion dollar National Debt, what would China really have to fear from an Obama candidacy as U.N. Secretary-General?

Additionally, what a deal for both Russia and China. Without spending a dime of their own, why not continue to keep the United States "pinned down" in the Middle East, Far East and Afghanistan by "allowing" our country to willingly continue to spill its blood and treasure - not only for its own National Security interests - but also, in effect, for China and Russia as well. Nevertheless, President Obama ironically chooses to tout, as meaningful major "concessions," 1) Russia (which has its own internal Islamic terrorist threat) "allowing" the United States to transport military equipment and supplies through its country to fight the Afghanistan War and 2) China's questionable and dubious cooperative efforts to exert its influence over a belligerent and irrational North Korea.

Although, considering the long-term perspective in the Middle East, it must also be remembered that there would be no Iranian nuclear weapons threat without 30 years of Russian nuclear technological complicity. And, regarding the turmoil and strife that has existed for decades in neighboring Afghanistan and Pakistan, both Russia and China benefit immensely by the United States' impetuous inclination to always fill the security void in that region for them, acting as "The World's Policeman."

Indeed, while the U.S. spent $2 Billion a week in Afghanistan, China spent that much and more in its proactive march towards securing future world economic dominance by cornering the market on mineral deposits worldwide. Illustratively, of what benefit is it for the United States to wean itself off imported oil by promoting electric battery-powered vehicles if China succeeds in cornering the worldwide market on lithium mineral deposits necessary to make the batteries?

Therefore, considering that Barack Obama has been President of the United States for two years, has his preference towards "conciliatory" diplomacy resulted in any more cooperation from either Russia or China on Iran or North Korea than President Bush got? Hardly. **As a consequence, even if both Russia and China were to acquiesce in the Security Council, exactly what would either**

country really have to fear from Barack Obama being named United Nations Secretary-General, given the results of President Obama's non-confrontational U.S. foreign policy espoused thus far?

And for those who may still believe that an Obama U.N. Secretary-General candidacy is out of the realm of possibility, who would have guessed that the members of the Nobel Peace Prize Selection Committee – a political mirror image of the prevailing consensus of Multinational thought of United Nations member states - would have bestowed the Nobel Peace Prize upon a President of the United States less than nine months into his presidency for, essentially, "just being there."

CHAPTER 2

9 *Barack Obama's "Ultimate End Game"* Ibid - Chapter 18; Pages 263-291.

10 *Wall Street Journal* – September 29, 2009.

11 *What Obama and the Democrats Knew That McCain Didn't* by Gary Patterson (Copyright 2009) Pages 195-196.

12 Even after the 20-month nadir of his Presidency, an October 2010 Gallup poll revealed that, clearly, still 91% of Black Voters support President Obama. Source: *L.A. Times* "New Gallup Findings for Democrats: Blacks Still Love Obama" by Andrew Malcomb – October 4, 2010. Further, regarding the Latino Vote, one need only look at the 2010 Democrat Senate wins in Nevada (15% Latino) and Colorado (12% Latino) where the Latino Vote was, indeed, the margin of victory in both states.

13 And, regarding the Black Vote, short of President Obama committing an Act of Treason or Condoleezza Rice appearing somewhere on the 2012 Republican Presidential ticket, it is likely that President Obama will again garner at least 90-95% of the Black Vote in 2012.

14 It is understood that the electoral vote, rather than the popular vote, determines presidential elections. However, it is the popular vote - on a state by state basis - that determines the winner of all the electoral votes in virtually every state (except for Nebraska and Maine which allocate electoral votes proportionately).

15 Only White Independents are considered in this Voter demographic "swing" group given that Blacks, almost unanimously voted for Obama in 2008 - even if some may identify themselves as Independent Voters.

16 *ABC News* "The Number" by Gary Langer – November 3, 2010.

17 *Barack Obama's "Ultimate End Game"* Ibid – Page 277. Having been elected President, many believed that America was entering a "Post-Racial" Era with Barack Obama as the human embodiment of a symbolic bridge - being born of a White mother and Black father. Sadly, Obama ceded that mantel of racial impartiality just six months into his Presidency with his visceral denunciation of the Cambridge Police without admittedly first "know[ing] all the facts." Indeed, had an alien visited earth and observed only the events relating to Professor Gates' arrest that week and the President's premature response to it, the last thing the alien would have ever guessed was that Barack Obama was also half White.

18 And, based on the current timetable of five-year terms, the United Nations

Secretary-General position should come open about the time President Obama would leave office in early 2017.

19 United Nations Security Council (www.unsg.org/role.html).

20 *Barack Obama's "Ultimate End Game"* Ibid – Page 282. Ironically, the combination of a) a rarefied I.Q.; b) never really having been criticized himself previously; c) not cognizant of his own limitations stemming from his own inexperience and d) ignoring the advice of experienced advisors which he, himself, selected, has militated against President Obama's ability at times to develop a perceptive acuity as it relates to the opinions of the average American Voter on issues of the day.

21 *Washington Post* "At the U.N., Many Hope for an Obama Win" by Colum Lynch - October 26, 2008.

22 United Nations Security Council (www.unsg.org/role.html) - Ibid.

Climate Change as the Top Priority of Obama and the United Nations

"My definition of [real] Leadership would be leading on Climate Change; an international accord that we'll potentially get in Paris [i.e. International Conference scheduled Nov. 30 – Dec 11, 2015]."
President Barack Obama – *60 Minutes* – October 11, 2015

More of President Barack Obama on Climate Change

"Yet, even as we meet threats like terrorism, we cannot and we must not ignore a peril that can effect generations. So I'm here today to say that Climate Change constitutes a serious threat to global security – an immediate risk to our National Security...denying it or refusing to deal with it endangers our National Security."

"Climate change will impact every country on the planet. No one is immune...Some warming is inevitable. But there comes a point when the worst effects will be irreversible. And time is running out...That's why confronting

Climate Change is now a key pillar of American global leadership."

President Barack Obama – U.S. Coast Guard Commencement Ceremony – New London, Connecticut – May 20, 2015 (Ironically ignoring as a National Security threat, just four days before, the major setback in the War against ISIS with the fall of the major city of Ramadi in Iraq)

Unequivocally, in 2015, according to Barack Obama, the Global Warming controversy, or Climate Change (as Environmentalists, Liberals and Democrats now fashion it to also conveniently encompass all meteorological calamities and even cold weather) is the single most important issue and U.S. National Security threat, domestic or foreign, facing our country. Although, ironically, the *Washington Post* noted "[I]t's hard to believe these days that during the 2012 campaign season, many liberal environmentalists were busy criticizing President Obama for his alleged 'climate silence' – his apparent unwillingness to talk about the chief issue facing our planet. By contrast, since re-election, he's been 'climate-outspoken' as you can imagine."[23] Now having "more flexibility," being beyond his "last election" undoubtedly had a lot to do with that. Nevertheless, the Republicans – joined by several Democrats from energy-producing states – criticize President Obama's domestic Climate Change agenda saying "he has gone too far" by drawing an equivalence between global warming and other moral and National Security priorities.[24]

Whereas United States Senator John Cornyn (R-TX), stating his belief as to what actually constitutes the greatest threat to our National Security in 2015 countered that *"People are coming from around the world through what they know is a porous [Southern] border to come to the United States without us knowing who they are or what their motives are. This is a National Security problem."* Further, U.S. Senator John Inhofe (R-Okla) derided President Obama: *"The President's speech at the National Coast Guard Academy stating his belief that Climate Change poses the greatest threat to future generations is a severe disconnect from reality."* **Well, apparently not according to the United Nations.**

Previous quotes from U.N. Secretaries-General Kofi Annan and Ban Ki-moon argue (as does President Obama) that Climate Change is, indeed, the Top Priority in terms of problems facing the United Nations and the World:

1. *"You may represent different countries, but the challenges we face are common – Climate Change – we have to save the planet...and I hope there will be a strong commitment demonstrated by the leaders of the world. We will be able to address this Climate Change – the single most important challenge which we are facing these days."*
2. *"Every country is affected. There is no country that is safe."*
3. *"Just last week, the International Energy Agency released a report saying we are close to a point of no return [on Climate Change]."*
4. *"Climate Change is a global problem requiring a global solution, global solidarity."*
   Current U.N. Secretary-General Ban Ki-moon – "The Human Impact of Climate Change" – Dhaka, Bangladesh - November 14, 2011
5. *"This is not some nation's historical responsibility. It is about all of our responsibility to future generations."*

6. *"[Climate Change success] will rise and fall on the strength of U.S. engagement and leadership. America is the world's biggest producer of greenhouse gases. It is also the planet's leading innovator. If it steps up to the plate, others will follow."*
U.N. Secretary-General Ban Ki-moon – "Event: Climate Change - The Defining Challenge"- Washington, DC – July 16, 2007

"I really appreciate such strong leadership and cooperation and support of the United States government and President Obama...On Climate Change, I intend to work very closely with the member states so that the legally binding global treaty can be achieved by the end of 2015...I intend to convene a leaders meeting sometime next year. I have invited President Obama. I invite him to play a very important role for humanity."
Ban Ki-moon – Remarks: White House Meeting with President Obama – April 11, 2013

"I believe we have a responsibility not only to our contemporaries but also to future generations – a responsibility to preserve resources that belong to them as well as to us; and without which none of us can survive."
Then-U.N. Secretary-General Kofi Annan – Farewell Speech – Independence, MO – December 11, 2006

"[After leaving office] I would want to work on some of the African issues, some of the human rights issues and the global governance and global warming issues."
Then-U.N. Secretary-General Kofi Annan – Final Press Conference – United Nations Headquarters, New York, NY – December 19, 2006

> *"Climate Change is the biggest challenge of our time."*
> Kofi Annan, former U.N. Secretary-General – January 2014[25]

Comparisons - Quoted Code Words/Phrases:

Ban Ki-moon and Kofi Annan U.N. Secretaries-General	Barack Obama U.S. President
1. *"Every country is affected. There is no country that is safe."*	*"Climate change will impact every country on the planet. No one is immune."*
2. *"...we are close to a point of no return [on Climate Change]."*	*"But there comes a point when the worst effects will be irreversible. And time is running out."*
3. *"...we have a responsibility to future generations."*	*"...a peril that can effect generations."*
4. *"[Climate Change success] will rise and fall on the strength of U.S. engagement and leadership."*	*"...climate change is now a key pillar of American global leadership."*
5. *"...Climate Change is the biggest challenge of our time."*	*...Climate Change constitutes an immediate threat to our National Security."*

Moreover, based on recent statements, even today the issue of Climate Change remains, steadfastly, the top global priority of both former United Nations Secretary-General Kofi Annan and current U.N. Secretary-General Ban Ki-moon:

1. Question: What is your greatest fear for the planet in the future?

    "That the world is reaching the tipping point beyond which Climate Change may become irreversible."
    Kofi Annan – May 3, 2015[26]

2. *"World leaders agreed that Climate Change is a defining issue of our time and that bold action is needed today to reduce emissions and build resilience and that they would lead this effort."*
    Ban Ki-moon – United Nations Climate Summit: Final summary – September 25, 2014

3. "The Secretary-General (Ban Ki-moon) has fought tirelessly to ensure that Climate Change stays at the top of (world) leaders' agendas and has launched a number of initiatives to fight Climate Change on the ground to mobilize Climate Change...The Secretary-General is working with governments to meet their agreement to mobilize $100 Billion per year by 2020..."
    United Nations View: Climate Change –The U.N. and Climate Change: Secretary-General "Leading on Climate Change" – January 31, 2015

Contrast Importance of Climate Change: As Viewed by the American People

A. Whereas President Obama insists *"that Climate Change constitutes a serious threat to global security – an immediate risk to our National Security,"* in stark contrast, in terms of the relative importance of immediate major issue priorities (i.e. what really matters most), in a 2014 opinion poll conducted by *Gallup* (March 6-9, 2014),the American People ranked Climate Change no better than 14th out of 15 major concerns as follows:[27]

1.	The Economy	59%
2.	Federal Spending and the Deficit	58%
3.	Health Care	57%
4.	Unemployment	49%
5.	Size/Power of the Federal Government	48%
6.	Social Security System	46%
7.	Hunger and Homelessness	43%
8.	Crime	39%
9.	Future Terrorist Attacks	39%
10.	Energy Availability and Affordability	37%
11.	Drug Use	34%
12.	Illegal Immigration	33%
13.	Environmental Quality	31%
14.	CLIMATE CHANGE	24%*
15.	Race Relations	17%

*Moreover, a majority of Americans polled said they were concerned about Climate Change "only a little" or "not at all."

A. Similarly, nine months later in December 2014, the *PBS News Hour* reported that recent polls - separately taken by Associated Press/NORC and another conducted by Yale University - disclosed that although "issues such as global warming and the Keystone XL Oil Pipeline are 'front-burner' for politicians, the AP/NORC and Yale polls show that they are not top-line issues for many Americans..."

Finally, specifically regarding the Keystone XL Pipeline, of those Americans who expressed a "strong opinion," 63% were in favor of approving it "…despite protests waged by environmental groups, and the political showdowns on the issues."[28] **Note that the results of these polls dovetail with the consensus of polls held on this issue in recent years wherein typically clearly 6 of 10 Americans remain in favor of building the Keystone Pipeline.**

Throughout the first seven years of his Presidency, many had wondered about the dilemma faced by President Obama as to whether he would ultimately side with Environmentalists, a key Democrat constituency that fervently opposed the Keystone Pipeline or Labor Unions - Obama's second largest political donor - that favored approving the pipeline's construction and the jobs it would create. However, given President Obama's penchant and priority for placating United Nations Climate Change policy and Ban Ki moon in particular regarding all climate issues, it was ultimately no dilemma at all for Barack Obama to reject the Keystone Pipeline in November 2015. In reality, the Labor Unions never really stood a chance. President Obama just had to delay his rejection decision until after the last federal election of his Presidency in 2014.

B. In recent years a number of the national polling services have, alternatively chosen to highlight how even a majority of Republicans are embracing the idea of the United States working towards reducing the amount of man-made carbon emissions in the atmosphere. Yet, in the abstract, if there were absolutely no cost burden in reducing carbon emissions, who on this planet wouldn't be in favor of the cleanest air possible? Candidly, the more salient question is: "At what cost do the American People support the reduction of carbon emissions?" **When considering the cost of actually**

paying for reducing carbon emissions by increasing the tax burden to Americans, the enthusiasm for reducing carbon emissions – even among Democrats – is not as robust; dropping off considerably.

Illustratively, in its July 2014 Report (#13), the *National Surveys on Energy and Environment* heralded the statistic that 60 percent of Americans, including 51% of Republicans, were in favor of using carbon tax revenue to support research and development funding for renewable energy programs. It was further noted in the report that a majority of Americans support a carbon tax so long as it is revenue-neutral (i.e. it doesn't cost anything) or if all the carbon tax revenue collected were to be returned to them in the form of tax rebate checks (again, if it doesn't cost anything). The survey report (as they interpreted it) signaled the increase in support as a major shift in recognition and acceptance among Americans, across the political spectrum, for imposing a tax to reduce carbon emissions.

However, revealingly ("where the rubber meets the road"), in the only survey question of five wherein *a specific out-of-pocket carbon tax cost* was put to those surveyed (i.e. a 10% increase in their energy bills), the respondents, in fact, *opposed* imposing any federal carbon tax by a decisive margin of 68% to 29% - nearly 7 in 10 – including Democrats who also voted it down 56% to 41%:

Specifically, "the survey asked about support for 'a carbon fuel tax that significantly lowered greenhouse gases but increased your energy costs by 10% a month.'"

Moreover, based on the 2009 Energy bill as passed by the then-Democrat-controlled House of Representatives, *The Heritage Foundation* projected that 1) utility costs for a family of four would increase by $829 per year (rising vastly more than 10%) and 2) a gallon of gasoline would cost $1.38 per gallon more.[29]

C. The partisan-Democrat *Center for American Progress* lamented that "President Obama took office with four major domestic agenda items (including) clean energy and global warming legislation to create jobs, reduce oil use, and cut pollution. The President succeeded on the first three (domestic agenda items). But clean energy legislation died in the Senate after passing in the House."[30] But why?

As a candidate and as President, Barack Obama has emphatically supported the idea of carbon taxes to compel Americans to reduce carbon emissions. In particular, during Barack Obama's initial year in office, when the Democrats controlled the Presidency as well as both houses of Congress, the House of Representatives, in fact, passed legislation to that effect. However, the Senate Majority Leader Harry Reid, who throughout the first six years of the Obama Presidency invariably did the President's bidding in the Senate, ultimately refused to bring the Democrat-controlled House of Representatives carbon tax bill to the floor of the Democrat-controlled Senate for consideration.

Essentially because of the unknown potential long-term financial and political toxicity as to how Americans would react ahead of the 2010 Mid-Term elections, this was the only instance wherein Senator Reid ever withheld from

Senate consideration a major bill passed by the Democrat-controlled House of Representatives. And remember: Given that the Democrats controlled both Houses of Congress as well as the Presidency, there would have been absolutely no barriers as to its passage had the Democrats really wanted it.

Arguably, one could reasonably conclude that President Obama, even at a time during the first year of his Presidency when he enjoyed robust popularity, must have had second thoughts, politically, about going forward with carbon tax legislation in the Senate in 2010 – a Mid-Term election year with the country still reeling from the 2008-2009 recession. Otherwise during the 2009-2010 period, it is hard to believe that Senator Reid would have suddenly been "calling the shots" and have stood in the way of President Obama - if the President truly wanted the House carbon tax bill passed at that time.

Obama's EPA Bona fides

Rather than legislative, probably what President Obama will view as his most enduring environmental and Climate Change achievement was realized through regulation – based on the edicts of the Environmental Protection Agency (EPA) imposed over the past seven years which, no doubt he will continue to pursue and tout.

Although, based on a 2014 study conducted by the *National Association of Manufacturers*, federal regulations impose a cost to the American People and consumers of over $2 Trillion per year. **Moreover, in addition to that $2 Trillion amount, in 2014 alone, the Obama Administration's EPA imposed new regulations that are estimated – on the low end – to cost an additional $200 Billion a year more into perpetuity; or an environmental cost** increase to the American People of at least 10 percent in just one year. However, the United Nations undoubtedly would take note and laud Mr. Obama for his efforts.

> According to data compiled by the Federal government's *Regulations.gov* website (and gleaned) by the *Daily Caller,* most of the new regulatory schemes involve energy and the environment – 139 during a mere two-week period in December 2014, to be precise. In all, the Obama Administration foisted more than 75,000 pages of regulations on the United States in 2014.[31]

But the EPA Fails to Consider Cost of Regulations

In June 2015, the Supreme Court ruled against the EPA citing that, in imposing its regulatory authority, it had violated the law by purposely failing to consider the requisite factor of cost to those individuals and companies who must comply with new regulations:

> Dealing a blow to White House efforts to curb pollution, the Supreme Court ruled the Obama Administration acted improperly when it decided to regulate power plant emission of mercury and other toxic air pollutants...At issue in *Utility Air Regulatory Group v. EPA* is whether the environmental agency properly considered industry-compliance costs when deciding to adopt rules – or if its regulators instead unfairly emphasized the public benefits. In its ruling, the Supreme Court said:
>
> *"The [EPA] must consider cost – including, most importantly, cost of compliance – before deciding whether regulation is appropriate and necessary."*[32]

Similarly, in 2014, on this very issue this author wrote:[33]

> **Either engrained or purposeful, the rule-making bureaucrat is prone to neglect the requisite dual consideration as to the cost of practical implementation of those new regulations that might, otherwise, "kill" them – i.e. that being the specific prohibitive impact of unreasonable and excessive cost and time that such regulations may unjustly engender and impose on those individuals and businesses affected.**
>
> **Understanding the "Death Star" Lifecycle of Federal Regulatory Bureaucracies:**
>
> The inherent nature of bureaucracies makes one both skeptical and wonder that, at some point, whether – after the first 29 years in the case of the EPA – the impetus for the vast majority of incremental regulation since 1998 has been primarily driven more by bureaucratic inertia and a need for self-perpetuation of a burgeoning and bloated workforce; rather than any substantial incremental need for further environmentally protective measures that can truly be justified.
>
> Understand: In a generic sense, regulatory agencies consist of two functions – a regulatory rule-making function and a regulatory enforcement function. If you're a rule-making bureaucrat, you're "in it for the long-haul" - i.e. a pension-for-life after 30 years. However, without new rules and regulations, what further need is there for the Regulatory rule-making function – or, alternatively, maybe only a downsized one at most? Accordingly, unless the lifetime bureaucrat is closing in on 30 years in the near future,

regulatory rule-making bureaucrats are, consciously or unconsciously, predisposed to inordinately look for reasons to generate even more regulations.

Thus, even if all environmental regulation subsequent to September 1998 were suspended, all Environmental Regulation during the first 29 years of existence (1970-1998) of the EPA, for example, would still be preserved and remain in effect.

Consequently, no one is talking about "gutting" the EPA here. Rather, just applying common sense and non-partisanship, the assumption being made here is that 29 years should have been ample time for the EPA to "get it done" – or damn near 100% done. Especially if one were to presume - from a Democrat's perspective – that the last six years of that 29-year period (i.e. 1993-1998) occurred on "the watch" of a Democrat President, Bill Clinton, who, most certainly, would have "rectified" and more than made up for "all the inattentiveness" of the Reagan - Bush (41) years (1981-1992) to Environmental concerns.

Nevertheless, even though the Supreme Court ruled against him in 2015, in a Machiavellian sense President Obama worked his will and won anyway. In that, pragmatically, most of the coal-fired power plants affected by this EPA regulation did not have the luxury of time to just stand by and wait for the possibility of a favorable Supreme Court ruling. In particular, given the requisite lead time that would have been necessary to comply, most of those power plants had already been compelled to commit to begin the unjust costly implementation of the EPA regulation anyway, long before the Supreme Court ruling.

Ultimately, regardless of the relative trace importance Americans attached to Climate Change and Environmental issues overall in 2014 (i.e. 14th and 13th, respectively, out of 15 National issues considered), expect Barack Obama to continue and accelerate environmental regulation on all fronts throughout the remainder of his Presidency - further ingratiating himself with both former U.N. Secretary-General Kofi Annan and current U.N. Secretary-General Ban Ki-moon. After all, President Obama is now beyond his "last Election" and, as he told then-Russian Prime Minister Dmitri Medvedev, in 2012, he "will have more flexibility" to do anything he wants.

To wit, *just one month after* the Supreme Court ruled against him (on June 30th, 2015), President Obama, undeterred, pressed forward - announcing (on August 2, 2015) even more stringent EPA regulations imposed against coal-fired power plants that the agency has freely admitted to in the past would most likely put many of such power plants eventually out of business. However, to be sure, this time the EPA will not be so cavalier as to make the mistake again of ignoring the requirement that it first perform at least a perfunctory cost/benefit analysis – which it did. To that end, the agency concocted its own self-serving calculation of a projected rarified $54 Billion benefit to consumers versus a power plant implementation compliance cost of only $8.4 Billion.

Although, this latest attempt by President Obama's EPA apparently did not go unnoticed by a majority of the Supreme Court, which in February 2016 issued an unprecedented stay blocking these newest regulations issued in August 2015 by the EPA against coal-fired power plants. Nevertheless, even if ultimately President Obama doesn't prevail, he would still benefit by further ingratiating himself - in the eyes of U.N. Secretary-General Ban Ki-moon and the United Nations - with merely the attempt.

CHAPTER 3

23 *Washington Post* "Not Even Obama's National Security Argument Can Get Partisans to Agree on Climate Change" by Chris Mooney – May 22, 2015.

24 *Washington Times* "Obama: Climate Change a Threat to Homeland Security, Hurts Military Readiness" by Ben Wolfgang – May 20, 2015.

25 U.S. House Committee on Energy and Commerce "Rep. Waxman and Sen. Whitehouse Criticize Republican Leaders for Climate Change Response" - February 20, 2014.

26 *The Guardian* "Kofi Annan: 'We Must Challenge Climate Change Sceptics Who Deny the Facts'" by Nicola Davis – May 3, 2015.

27 *Gallup Polling* "Climate Change Not a Top Worry in the U.S." by Rebecca Riffkin – March 12, 2014.

28 Polls: *PBS NewsHour* "Half of Republicans Back Limits on Carbon Emissions, Poll Finds" by Dina Cappiello – December 12, 2014: Note that the poll reported that of "those with strong opinions," 31% were in favor and 18% opposed; with the remainder (51%) being "neutral or not sure" (i.e. Re: The calculated 63% figure "in favor" - Considering only those with "strong opinions," 31% in favor divided by 49% (31% in favor plus 18% opposed = 49% total). Thus, those respondents with "strong opinions" favored approving the Keystone Pipeline = 63% (31%/49%).

29 *The Heritage Foundation* "The Economic Consequences of Waxman-Markey: An Analysis of the American Clean Energy and Security Act of 2009" by Wm. W. Beach, Karen Campbell Ph.D., David W. Kreutzer Ph.D., Ben Lieberman and Nicolas Loris – August 6, 2009.

30 *Center for American Progress* "Anatomy of a Senate Climate Bill Death" by Daniel J. Weiss – October 12, 2010.

31 www.thenewamerican.com "Obama Imposed 75,000 Pages of new Regulations in 2014" by Alex Newman – December 30, 2014.

32 *International Business Times* – "Supreme Court Ruled Against EPA Mercury and Air Toxic Standards For US Coal Plants" by Maria Galluci and Ginger Gibson – June 29, 2015.

33 *America at the Precipice* - Ibid – Pages 353-354.

President Obama Relentlessly Currying Favor with U.N. Muslim Nation States and Why

President Obama's Refusal to use the term "Islamic Extremism"

> *"We [the United Nations] are developing a comprehensive plan to prevent **Violent Extremism.** Last month, I convened religious leaders from around the world at the United Nations to promote tolerance, reconciliation and dialogue."* Ban Ki-moon, U.N. Secretary-General – Remarks upon receiving an Honorary Degree from the Catholic University at Leuvin (Belgium) – May 25, 2015

In fact, beginning as far back as 2011 with the formation of the multi-lateral group Global Counterterrorism Forum (GCTF) and the subcommittee Working Group called Countering Violent Extremism; the United Nations formally began its focus on the revised nomenclature of "Violent Extremism"[34] - thereafter assiduously avoiding the use or religious reference to the term "Islamic Extremism."

However, with the advance of ISIS well into Iraq and the Charlie Hebdo-Jewish Delicatessen terrorist massacre in Paris in early 2015, President Obama was roundly criticized by Republicans and a handful of Democrats for his response to both events – by refusing to use the term, "Islamic Extremism" or "Islamic Terrorism" to describe the self-proclaimed Islamic terrorists, who committed their atrocities and proudly claimed credit for them during the attack. Indeed, the admitted first and foremost motivation sworn to by the assassins was their professed allegiance and devotion to Islam and Allah. However, to the contrary, President Obama insisted:

> *"We must never accept the premise that they [ISIS] put forward because it is a lie. They are not religious leaders. They are terrorists...What I do insist on is that we maintain a proper perspective and we do not provide a victory to these terrorist networks by overinflating their importance and suggesting in some fashion that they are an existential threat to the United States or the world order...I think we do ourselves a disservice in this fight if we are not taking into account the fact that the overwhelming majority of Muslims reject this ideology."*
>
> President Barack Obama – February 18, 2015 at the White House Summit on "Countering Violent Extremism"

Pope Francis' Belief that ISIS is Motivated by Religious Intolerance

Juxtapose President Obama's refusal to use the term "Islamic Extremism" against Pope Francis, who - that same month - emphatically condemned the beheading of 21 Coptic Christians by the Islamic State (ISIS) for no other reason than, according to the Pope, "because they were Christians."[35] Moreover, Pope Francis six months earlier (August 2014) had already endorsed and believed it justified to use military force "to counter unjust aggression" committed by ISIS Islamic fanatics who had savagely attacked and killed thousands of Christians "simply for their religious beliefs."[36] And although he was silent as to the Pope's position on this very issue, by contrast, President Obama seems to never miss publically claiming Pope Francis' endorsement on issues that Mr. Obama favors (e.g. Climate Change and ending Cuban isolation).

Even Muslim King Abdullah of Jordan and General el-Sisi of Egypt have no misgivings about labelling the ISIS threat as virulent Islamic Terrorism.

RE: Terrorism: Obama's Verbatim Adoption of U.N. Nomenclature

Yet, in February 2015, President Obama insisted upon choosing the exact nomenclature previously adopted years earlier in 2011 by the United Nations to substitute any reference to Islamic terrorism for "Violent Extremism," in naming the White House conference on terrorism "The summit on Countering *Violent Extremism*" – also attended by U.N. Secretary-General Ban Ki-moon. In fact, the exact summit title – Countering Violent Extremism – was "lifted" verbatim by President Obama from the name of the United Nations subcommittee Working Group entitled *Countering Violent Extremism*.

However, never really picking up on this United Nations connection, the Conservative and Liberal media were both collectively left wondering from where President Obama had suddenly come to be using the particular term, *Violent Extremism* to henceforth describe Islamic Terrorism.

The Literal Apocalyptic Koran Interpretation Adopted by ISIS[37]

It should be noted that a 2012 *Pew Research Poll* of more than 38,000 face-to-face interviews of Muslims worldwide revealed that, in 32 out of 39 Muslim Nations, "half or more Muslims say there is only one correct way to understand the teachings of Islam" – dismissing the literal interpretation of the Koran as espoused by ISIS and other extremist terrorist groups. So, President Obama was correct when he asserted that *"the overwhelming majority of Muslims reject this ideology."*

However, the remaining seven out of 39 Muslim Nations do, in fact, "believe that it is possible to interpret Islam's teachings in multiple ways" - including not only traditional but literal/"hardline" interpretations which – like ISIS - espouse:

1. All infidels and "non-believers" should be killed (if they will not submit or convert);

2. To actively work towards an apocalyptic, "end of days" scenario wherein only the true believers in Mohammed will remain and all others will perish and

3. (Lest we not forget), the 72 virgins that await those who die as martyrs for the cause.

But here's the problem: Those seven remaining Muslim Nations wherein "majorities or substantial minorities" exist and this literal apocalyptic interpretation of the Koran predominantly flourishes are located in the Middle East and North-Africa. Moreover, three other countries not included in the 2012 *PewResearch* survey where this literal apocalyptic interpretation of the Koran exists are also located in the Middle East and North Africa region: Specifically, Iran, Iraq and Yemen. Conspicuously, it is essentially from these ten countries in which the most virulent Radical Islamic Extremist element predominantly nests and from where they export their trademark brand of brutal terrorism now worldwide.

Further, although at mortal war with each other, both Sunnis and Shiites hold the belief that the "End of Times" prophecies are today finally at hand. Specifically, the "End of Times" prophecies center upon an apocalyptic "Grand Battle" to be fought in Syria that will precede the "End of Times" and usher in Muslim world domination. The problem is that both the Sunni and Shiite sects welcome this "Grand Battle" and death - certain that each is the true-believers of Allah and will be chosen to reign supreme with their Leader throughout eternity.

One could further reasonably argue that it is presumptuous for Barack Obama, a self-proclaimed Christian, to assume the mantel of final arbiter and authority on the motives and beliefs of Muslims worldwide; further pontificating as to his expertise on and interpretation of the Koran. **Second, as to his insistence that ISIS and their ilk are merely perverting the Koran and are not true-believers, how does he then explain that ISIS suicide bombers are enthusiastically dying for something that, according to Mr. Obama, they have to know to be, in reality, an utter fraud?**

Specifically, the discussion of the primary issue that follows has absolutely nothing to do with 1) Barack Obama in any way being hostile towards Christianity or 2) the wholly unsubstantiated notion that he is a Muslim himself. Rather, it centers upon Obama's *original thought-process* and to what extent was it possibly influenced by United Nations policy:

> **A. When did he first formulated his contentious position that there is absolutely no legitimate linkage whatsoever between the Islamic religion and the terrorist acts** committed by self-proclaimed Muslim military and para-military groups who swear their allegiance to Allah, and

B. Why he subsequently shifted to using the term *Violent Extremism."*

Specifically: **1) Was it Barack Obama's original idea or someone else's and 2) If not, whose idea was it and what was Mr. Obama's real motivation for adopting it?**

One must remember that, although only a few Democrats openly dared to differ with President Obama on his refusal to use the term "Islamic Extremism," Mr. Obama was pretty much out there on his own - as very few leading Democrats outside the Administration rushed to support or reiterate the President's contention. Given that polls in early 2015 revealed a significant majority of Americans believed President Obama's War against ISIS was already going poorly, rank and file Democrats saw no upside for President Obama to be perceived as looking even weaker on U.S. foreign policy – by refusing to label ISIS or the perpetrators of terrorist acts throughout the world (like the Paris Charlie Hebdo-Jewish Delicatessen terrorist attacks) as "Islamic Extremists" (indeed, even though praising Allah while carrying out their murderous acts).

In the absence of any other consideration, even Democrats were left to wonder why President Obama appeared to be playing a game of semantics - proactively choosing to envelop himself in a controversy of choice that, politically, 1) could only exacerbate his already perceived political weakness in conducting U.S. foreign policy while, simultaneously, 2) dragging his political party down with him. Further, there is also a downside for Democrats wherein their President, no longer facing re-election himself is now unfettered (i.e. "After my (2012) Election, I will have more flexibility.") to potentially continue pursuing a still unannounced, separate political legacy ambition of his own. Namely, although Barack Obama has a stake in his political party's success in 2016, there potentially remains a higher order to his personal legacy priorities: one day becoming the Secretary-General of the United Nations.

Secondly, by showcasing himself to the world as eschewing all linkages and reference to the Islam religion and terrorism, President Obama could only be perceived in a more favorable light by the Muslim nations of the world. Of course, there is a political downside in that the American People, who already perceive President Obama's foreign policy performance as questionable at best, will most probably interpret his continued reticence to utter the words "Islamic terrorism" or "Islamic extremism" in the face of future attacks as only reinforcing that narrative.

Thirdly, many were stunned that President Obama chose not to join virtually every prominent world leader in Paris, France to march hand-in-hand in support of the French people on the Sunday following the terrorist attacks. White House Press Secretary Josh Ernest cited inadequate time to arrange security as to why President Obama could not attend even though leaders from 50 other nations – including Israeli President Netanyahu and Palestinian President Mahmoud Abbas - managed to show up. Even CNN's Fareed Zakaria – from whom Obama has personally sought out advice in the past – believed the President's absence was a mistake on his part.

But, even if President Obama refused to attend, at least as a minimum diplomatic courtesy, why did he also deliberately choose not to send some high-ranking official in his absence like Vice President Biden (isn't that exactly the kind of thing that Vice-Presidents do?), Secretary of State Kerry and/or then-Attorney General Eric Holder, who just happened to be in Paris that very day? Or could it possibly have been that the President's primary motivation was his concern as to the optics of his presence there in the eyes of United Nations Muslim nations. And if it was for any other reason than his penchant for avoiding - at all cost – even the possibility of offending Muslim United Nations member states, one would think that President Obama should have no misgivings about telling the American People exactly what it was.

Yet, if Mr. Obama truly intends to, one day, seek the position of United Nations Secretary-General after leaving the White House, is it not a higher personal political priority for him to continue to be seen on the world stage as an undaunted advocate on behalf of all Muslim nations? Bluntly, given that Barack Obama is passed the last Federal election, from purely a *personal* political perspective, during the final two years of his Presidency, does it really matter to him what the American People may think of him on this specific issue?

The North Carolina Killings of Three Muslim Students

Although triple murders too frequently occur somewhere in the United States (at times even in President Obama's own adopted home town of Chicago), in the triple murder of three Muslim students in Chapel Hill, North Carolina in February 2015, President Obama felt it this time incumbent upon himself to publically denounced these killings in particular. And, although he did not specifically call it a "hate crime," Mr. Obama clearly inferred it when he felt compelled to add *"No one in the United States should ever be targeted because of who they are, what they look like, or how they worship."*

Specifically, just three days after the shootings, President Obama, presumably, chose to prematurely seize upon the unsubstantiated belief of the father of one of the murder victims that the motivation of the killer, an admitted atheist, strongly suggested a religious-hate crime. When, in fact, based on the police investigation of witnesses thus far – including the killer's wife and several neighbors – the murders were, rather, a tragic and senseless culmination of a long-running dispute over an apartment building parking space.

By contrast, it is more than just coincidence that, in 2015, when eight Oregon college students and an instructor were shot dead for courageously declaring their Christian faith when confronted by a crazed gunman, President Obama never emphasized or, for that matter, even mentioned once that these murder victims were also "targeted because of…how they worship." Not a word. But there is no incentive. It does nothing to further his political agenda.

Rather President Obama saw the tragedy as a vehicle to "politicize" and direct his outrage towards yet another aspect of the Democrat mantra: Gun Control. Whereas had the victims been Muslim, given the President's previously demonstrated Modus Operandi in North Carolina, most assuredly the subject of "religious intolerance against Muslims in America" would not have escaped his gaze.

Obama Exclusively Advancing his Agenda is "Un-Presidential"

As is his want, throughout his Presidency, Mr. Obama has repeatedly "leaped to justice," (or to the microphones) with what is now an observable pattern of his desire and trait to prematurely draw conclusions as to nefarious motives suggesting (consciously, or granting him the benefit of doubt, unconsciously) a desired outcome that fits his narrative for advancing his causes, beliefs and/or divisive political motives.

This repeated profile, unbecoming of the office of the President

of the United States, wherein Mr. Obama prematurely weighs in to suggest a narrative and sway early public opinion that, not coincidently, fits his agenda and/or preconceived beliefs, reveals an obvious attempt to influence outcomes and buttress his own political or preconceived positions on controversial issues. In this particular instance – by prematurely suggesting the victimization of the three Muslims for their religion as the potential motive for their murder - Mr. Obama elevates political considerations and agendas above legitimate concern nationwide in a potential effort to counter, or deflect, the repeated criticism, mostly from Republicans and Conservatives, that he is perceived as being weak or timid in his refusal to use the term "Radical Islamic Terrorism."

Illustratively throughout his Presidency, Mr. Obama has voluntarily and proactively inserted himself, for example, on the side of the black or minority victim i.e. 1) the Professor Gates/Cambridge (MA) Police arrest, 2) the Trayvon Martin self-defense shooting and 3) the Michael Brown/Ferguson, Missouri self-defense shooting – of which all three incidents were ultimately ruled to be justifiable arrests or homicides. Nevertheless, win or lose, with each incident, President Obama *politically succeeds* in reinforcing his "street-cred" and re-energizing (ginning up) his base constituencies.

Accordingly, President Obama knows (or may consciously or unconsciously hope) that, politically, an incident such as the North Carolina Triple Murder – if ultimately found to be a "hate crime" - will somehow deflect criticism from his controversial larger contention that Islamic Extremism plays absolutely no role in the motivation of Islamic terrorists. Although, in repeatedly advancing his own agenda and "ginning up" his political base, President Obama may be wise to heed his own words from his 2009 speech before the United Nations wherein he lectured from the podium:

"The test of our leadership will not be the degree to which we feed the fears and hatred of our people."

Finally, in a December 2015 interview with PBS, Obama chose to raise the specter of White racial prejudice again (i.e. his skin color) as a factor in his negative Presidential Approval ratings. Although, in the past – in an effort /disclaimer to deflect criticism of his playing the "victim" card – President Obama would tacitly acknowledge that he also has benefitted from Whites who, in fact, voted for him primarily because of his skin color. However, on this occasion, he chose *not* to acknowledge this fact (i.e. "White Guilt"), which arguably substantially offset any so-called Voter white prejudice against Barack Obama nationwide.

More significantly, a convincing case can be made that no American on the planet or in its history has benefitted more from 1) Affirmative Action and 2) because of his skin color than Barack Obama. Indeed, had Barack Obama been born with merely the same skin color of a White male in a country of 30+ million adult White males, purely from an objective statistical perspective, the odds of Barack Obama ever having become President would have been infinitetesimal. Therefore, President Obama advocating on behalf of minorities is one thing. But to have the temerity to also attempt to identify himself as a minority victim throughout his life of white prejudice is quite a stretch – rivaling Hillary Clinton pleading poverty after leaving the White House in 2001.

Moreover, even with his African-American heritage, one is left to wonder whether or how Barack Obama would or could have qualified academically to transfer to nationally prestigious and exclusive Columbia University from Occidental College - where it was also rumored that, scholastically, Obama's grades were less than stellar. Could this be why Barack Obama has refused to ever make his college academic records public?

Of course, we will never know because for some peculiar reason Mr. Obama is still personally and - more specifically - politically apprehensive about allowing anyone to see his college academic records. And the mainstream media essentially ignoring this issue further exemplifies its protective and incurious nature towards virtually any issue that could reflect negatively on Barack Obama.

Obama Silently Condones U.S. Sanctuary Cities

Similarly, throughout his Presidency, Mr. Obama has made known to the media personal telephone calls to individuals perceived as victims of "hot button" causes that, politically, he enthusiastically supports: i.e. Sandra Fluke (Free Contraception/The so-called "War on Women"); NBA player Jason Collins (Gay Rights), etc. President Obama even found time to publically laud a Muslim American boy from Texas - inviting him to the White House for his ingenuity in fashioning a "cool clock" with wires attached - making it appear like an explosive device and bringing it to school with him; to the alarm of school officials. But, do not expect President Obama to pick up the phone and personally call the parents of Kate Steinle, the 32-year-old San Francisco murder victim shot dead in July 2015 by a criminal illegal alien who had been deported on five previous occasions; yet illegally re-entered the U.S. each time.

As a "sanctuary city," San Francisco defiantly flaunts U.S. Federal Immigration law notification requirements. And in the case of Francisco Sanchez, the criminal alien and murderer, San Francisco Sheriff Ross Mirkarimi failed to notify ICE that his department had custody of Sanchez but subsequently released him to the streets. However, no matter how senseless and tragic, bluntly, for the Obama Administration to have acknowledged a murder by some- one who is a criminal illegal alien loose on the streets of America would only invite further criticism of 1) President Obama's weak border security agenda and 2) President Obama's condoning (by his continued silence) the liberal Democrat and United Nations "open borders" immigration rights mantra practiced by U.S. sanc- tuary cities, clearly in defiance of United States Immigration law.

As further exemplified by President Obama's Secretary of Homeland Security Jeh Johnson a week after the nationally publi- cized murder of Kate Steinle, Johnson inexplicably said he didn't even know who Kate Steinle was. Yet it was Johnson's own im- migration enforcement agency, ICE that made it known to San Francisco authorities that it wanted to arrest Francisco Sanchez before he was released to the streets and had the opportunity to kill Ms. Steinle.

Either Johnson was professionally negligent (living under a rock) or purposely lying which, albeit perjury, pleading ignorance is still the path of least resistance to avoid having to answer uncom- fortable Congressional inquiries, no matter how foolish one may temporarily appear. But frankly, for either Barack Obama or Jeh Johnson to acknowledge Ms. Steinle's murder by a criminal illegal alien does nothing to advance the narrative of favored Democrat causes - only drawing negative attention to them. It is, in essence, Standard Democrat Operating Procedure.

Secondly, nor for that matter should the courageous Baltimore mother, Toya Graham, expect a personal call from President Obama any time soon either. Specifically, on camera before the nation, in an act of demonstrated pure parental love and responsibility, Ms. Graham forcibly removed her teenage son from participating in any further nefarious and dangerous rioting activity. Nevertheless, Sandra Fluke warrants recognition and a call from the President, but Ms. Graham does not?

The U.N. (not Obama) Originated the Concept that Conflict is Political, Not Religious

Ultimately, remember that one of President Obama's primary requisites should he wish to one day become the United Nations Secretary-General is to continue ingratiating himself with A) both the current and former U.N. Secretaries-General, Ban Ki-moon and Kofi Annan, respectively and B) the United Nations Muslim states. **Moreover, the concept and premise that "the origin of conflict" is substantially political, and not religious, did not actually originate with Barack Obama, but with the then-United Nations Secretary-General Kofi Annan in 2006:**

> *"On the work of the Alliance of Civilizations [a U.N. Initiative meant to diffuse tension between Western and Muslim nations], one thing that came through very clearly is that some of the conflicts we are seeing – believing that it is religion which is at the basis, is not necessarily so.* Most of it is political policies and differences, which pushes some people sometimes to take the law into their own hands and go in another direction. *The issue is not faith. Yes, in some situations the faithful behave very badly towards each other, but the basis of most of these conflicts is political."*
> Kofi Annan, then-U.N. Secretary-General – Farewell Press Conference – December 19, 2006

However, to date, no one in the Media has demonstrated even a modicum of curiosity as to the motivation and origin of thought in the decision-making process that President Obama went through in what has turned out to be such a controversial issue. Presumably, the Media just assumed, consciously or unconsciously, that President Obama had arrived at his rationale for using the term, *Violent Extremism,* based upon an original thought of his own – never even considering the possibility that President Obama was once again initially motivated and influenced by prior United Nations policy positions and statements as an indicator or reflection of the thinking of the current and former U.N. Secretaries-General.

CHAPTER 4

34 *Countering Radicalisation and Violent Extremism Among Youth to Prevent Terrorism* – Veenkamp and S Zieger – Page 152 -- https://books.google.com/books?isbn =1614994706 – M. Lombardi, E Ragab, V. Chin – 2014 – (business and economics).

35 *CNSNews.com* "White House Avoids Mentioning that 21 Beheaded were Christians" by Patrick Goodenough – February 16, 2015.

36 *The Daily Mail* "Using Force against Iraqi Extremists is Justified Says Pope: Francis Backs Military Action to Stop Persecution of Christians by Islamic Fanatics" by Jason Groves – August 18, 2014.

37 1) *Pew Research* "The World's Muslims: Unity and Diversity – Executive Summary" www.pewforum.org – August 9, 2012. 2) *Reuters* "Apocalyptic Prophecies Drive Both Sides to Syrian Battle for End of Times" by Miriam Karouny – April 4, 2014.

How Obama's Immensely Unpopular Amnesty for Illegals Executive Order Mirrors Recklessly-Naïve U.N. Policy

Conservative critics contend that Barack Obama's quasi-Open Door and loose U.S. Border Security Immigration policy is singularly driven by his desire to create a future permanent underclass of American Voters who will be dependent upon, and thus beholden to the Democrat Party. True or not, it can equally be argued that the imposition of such Immigration policies that mirror those promulgated by the United Nations will correspondingly provide the ancillary boost to any personal political legacy ambition of President Obama, should he wish to, one day, become the next United Nations Secretary-General.

Specifically, what is to follow is a comparison and analysis of United Nations stated policy on Immigration and in support of granting refugee status (and therefore asylum) to both minors and adults who enter the United States illegally - which, again, not only mirrors but appears to have guided the actions (or perhaps more specifically inaction) and policy decisions of Barack Obama, as President of the United States, on the question of illegal immigration in this country.

President Obama Announces Illegal Amnesty

To avoid further potential losses, Barack Obama waited until after the 2014 Mid-Term elections (i.e. but just ten days after) to finally announced what he had hinted about for months - that he was taking Executive Action, as President, to declare amnesty for as many as 4-5 million immigrants who had previously illegally crossed the border into the United States. In particular, approximately 3.7 million illegal immigrants would qualify if they have illegally been in the U.S. for at least five years (Presumably, the burden to prove an illegal alien has not been in the U.S. for five years will fall on the government). Another 900,000 would qualify, including children and the parents of those children who entered the country illegally. Further, all illegal immigrants who qualify would then be permitted to immediately apply for a Social Security Card and driver's license.

President Obama politically justified his authority to act, in his mind, based on what he termed as an intolerable delay on the part of the legislative branch - the Congress of the United States - to pass "comprehensive" Immigration reform. "After six years of often bitter back-and-forth with Congressional Republicans over the issue of Immigration, President Obama announced that he had decided to go it alone by temporarily shielding 5 million immigrants from being deported." Further, regarding law enforcement efforts going forward, Mr. Obama stated that the deportation of undocumented immigrants in the United States should solely focus upon *"Felons, not families. Criminals, not children."*[38]

Legal standing:
President Obama's Interpretation of the "Take Care Clause"

Whereas legally, the President's Office of Legal Counsel defended his Executive Action on Immigration as being consistent and in keeping with the "Take Care Clause" of the United States Constitution as to a President's responsibility to *take care that [all] the laws be faithfully executed.* " Specifically, in a memorandum, the Presidential Office of Legal Counsel reasoned that, although there are estimated to be 11.3 million illegal immigrants in the United States, Congress only provided funding to process and deport about 400,000. Ergo, President Obama was within the law to apply "prosecutorial discretion" to selectively prioritize enforcement of, in this case, only illegal immigrants with criminal records.

Although, how effective and beneficial can the Obama Administration's prioritized enforcement effort to arrest and deport criminal illegal aliens be to the American People when juxtaposed against the 195,900 criminal illegal aliens (arrested and detained during the Obama Presidency) who, at one time, were in custody but have since been released to the streets by ICE while awaiting deportation judgment? As a consequence, these criminals are currently roaming the country while they await deportation hearings that can take years to adjudicate. In fact, of the 36,007 Criminal illegal aliens released by ICE in 2013, over 1,000 of them – just one year later - have since "went on to commit new (felony) crimes ranging from assault with a deadly weapon and lewd acts with a child to aggravated assault, robbery and hit-and-run."[39]

Obama's Demonstrated Lack of Enthusiasm for Expediting the Deportation Process

Of course, the Obama Administration will blame 1) the courts for forcing ICE to release two-thirds of those 195,900 criminal illegal aliens and 2) the delay in reforming and expediting the Immigration judicial deportation process on a lack of funding by a Republican-controlled Congress. **However, Democrats conveniently ignore the**

fact that it was a Democrat-controlled Congress during the first two years of the Obama Administration when the President had free rein to pass any law he wished pertaining to Immigration funding to reform and expedite the deportation judicial process. But he chose not to. In fact, the Immigration judicial phase, which is integral to the deportation process, is under the purview and control of the Federal government that President Obama as the Chief Executive, thus controls and for which he alone, for the last seven years, has been responsible to find ways to expedite the process as well – assuming he really wanted to.

Nevertheless, if President Obama had, indeed, proactively sought the requisite funding to be specifically and only earmarked for revamping and expediting the Immigration Deportation process (e.g. adding the requisite number of judges, court personnel, etc.), a Republican-controlled Congress would not have hesitated in approving it immediately. However, in seven years as President, Mr. Obama has demonstrated virtually no enthusiasm or interest to request the requisite funding for such a specific remedy. Illustratively, regarding his July 2014 Immigration funding request, *U.S. News* reported:

> Obama has asked Congress to allocate nearly $4 Billion to address the surge of unaccompanied minors coming across the southern border. Much of this money, however, wouldn't go to deportation, but to cover housing costs and legal costs for more than 50,000 children who have already come this year.[40]

"The Take Care Clause" and the Courts

Two federal court challenges (in Pennsylvania and Texas) are currently wending their way through the Courts of Appeals and, most likely, will ultimately be decided before the Supreme Court. Those two court cases to date have ruled against the constitutionality of President Obama's Executive Action on Immigration and a Stay has been instituted blocking its implementation (Although the Obama Administration has been cited once already by the Federal Court for illegally failing to obey the Court Order). Illustratively, in one Federal District Court case ruling against President Obama, according to *National Review Online:*

> United States Federal Judge Arthur J. Schwab (Western District of Pennsylvania) "rejected the Administration's claim that Obama's non-enforcement of the immigration laws is a valid exercise of "prosecutorial discretion," stating *'President Obama's unilateral legislative action violates the Separation of Powers provided for in the United States Constitution, as well as the Take Care Clause, and therefore is unconstitutional.' "[41]*

And there truly is no ambiguity in the succinct, yet simple ten-word sentence that is the so-called "Take Care Clause," explicitly defining the President's responsibility to the American People and oath a President takes to uphold the United States Constitution: *He [the President]shall take care that the laws be faithfully executed.*

Second, according to the legal watchdog organization *Judicial Watch,* in the years leading up to President Obama's Executive Action on Immigration, the Obama Administration has engaged in a number of Immigration law changes through Executive Actions affecting hundreds of thousands of illegal immigrants already. Specifically, *Judicial Watch* defined President Obama's use of "stealth amnesty" to mean the use of Executive Actions for selective deportation, prosecutorial discretion and de facto amnesty practices. As an example,

Judicial Watch cited the 2011 rejection by Congress of President Obama's DREAM ACT legislation - relating to amnesty for all children who entered the U.S. along with their illegal immigrant parents - and how Mr. Obama then proceeded to effectively circumvent (i.e. by-pass) Congress:

> **Without any statute authority, then-Secretary of Homeland Security Janet Napolitano instructed Immigration officers to stop pursuing, prosecuting and deporting illegal immigrants ages 16-30. Absolutely contrary to Federal law,** these illegal aliens are, thus now invited to remain in the United States and are given a re-newable two-year work permit. Another recent Executive Action further illustrates the point. On November 13, 2013, (the Obama Administration's) United States Citizenship and Immigration Service, in effect, unilaterally re-wrote sections of the current Immigration law by granting certain illegal aliens so-called "parole-in-place" status, which will circumvent current law requiring for their immediate deportation.

Judicial Watch concludes "little wonder the situation at the border continues to deteriorate: President Obama is unwilling to faithfully enforce (U.S.) Federal Immigration laws while he attacks states trying to ameliorate the pernicious effects produced by the President's failure to enforce the law.[42]

Third, no less than the renown liberal law professor and scholar Jonathan Turley, in a March 9, 2014 commentary for the *Los Angeles Times* warned about the dangerous legal precipice that President Obama has created for this country, noting that his demonstrated contempt for U.S. Constitutional Authority, the Separation of Powers and his expansion of Executive Privilege *"would have shocked the framers of the Constitution."*[43]

Presidential Legal Hypocrisy

Ironically, as recently as just eight months before announcing his November 2014 Executive Order on Immigration (and at least 21 times before that), President Obama himself emphatically agreed and acknowledged that he, as President had *no* legal authority to by-pass Congress and – through Executive Action – grant permanent legal status to as many as 4-5 million illegal immigrants in the United States. For example:

> *"The biggest problem that we're facing now has to do with [then-President Bush] trying to bring more and more power to the Executive Branch and not go through Congress at all. And that's what I intend to reverse when I'm President of the United States of America."*
> Barack Obama – Presidential Candidate, during the 2008 Presidential Campaign

> *"Believe me – believe me, the idea of doing things on my own is very tempting…But that's not how – that's not how our system works. That's not how our democracy functions. That's not how our Constitution is written."*
> President Barack Obama – Speaking before the 2011 *National Council of La Raza*[44]

The American People Weigh In

Moreover, clearly disregarding the overwhelming 60 percent to 36 percent opposition by the American People to his arbitrary immigration action, President Obama was still unwavering in his support for amnesty for illegal immigrants. Indeed, the poll question of amnesty for illegals was the President's worst-rated public policy position. Similarly, by a 60% to 38% margin, respondents said that they disapproved of President Obama by-passing Congress by issuing an Executive Order. Moreover, reflective of the depth and breadth of opposition to the illegal amnesty issue: "The (60%) number matches many other polls, and results of a November 2014 ballot in Oregon where voters in a deeply blue state voted two-to-one to block a Democrat-backed law that would have given illegals drivers' licenses."[45]

Further, trend findings over time conducted by the Gallup polling organization similarly revealed substantial opposition and deep concern by the American People towards illegal immigration into this country and its potential future financial cost ramifications. The following polling data statistically reflects that deep concern and sentiment:[46]

1. *How much do you personally worry about Illegal Immigration?*

Date	Great Deal		Fair Amount		Worried Total		Worried Not at All
Mar. 2015	39%	+	24%	=	**63%**	vs.	**16%**

2. *How important is it to you that government takes steps this year to deal with: Controlling U.S. borders to halt the flow of Illegal Immigration to the United States?*

Date	Extremely Important		Very Important		Moderately Important		Important Total		Not That Important
Feb. 2014	43%	+	34%	+	16%	=	**93%**	vs.	**7%**

Obama Enforcing U.N.-Endorsed International Immigration Law (Not U.S. Law)

In reality, President Barack Obama is, indeed, in favor of enforcing Immigration law. Except the particular brand of Immigration law being imposed by Mr. Obama *is not* that of the United States, but emulates the recklessly-naïve fantasy-like worldview of *International Human Rights Immigration Law as* espoused and promulgated by the United Nations and, specifically, its U.N. Secretary-General, Ban Ki-moon.

In particular, the conspicuous distinction is that the United Nations naively and arbitrarily rejects outright the heightened concern of the United States and the American People that border security is, indeed, a National Security priority. Instead, according to the United Nations, the National Security argument is, rather, a pretext used by nations to purposely exploit the human rights of "migrants" who show up or cross international borders.

Moreover, rather than National Security, at the heart of the United Nations' human rights interpretation of International Immigration law is the belief that the rights and physical security of the individual foreign migrant must be the paramount concern of all nation states thus, trumping any National Security concerns – without exception. In fact, the United Nations unequivocally rejects the precept that an immigrant who illegally crosses an international border has even committed a crime.

Further, the United Nations specifically construes, under International law that those international border areas (i.e. a country's so-called designated Customs check points) between two countries are still subject to and bound by the application and adherence to International Immigration law – which, the U.N. contends supersedes the Immigration laws of any destination country (including the United States). As a consequence, according to the rationale of the United Nations in applying International Immigration law 1) the human rights of any immigrant, as to protection and security, cannot ever be deprived nor 2) can a crime ever have been committed by the mere act of an immigrant crossing an international border, with or without the knowledge or permission of the destination country…Believe it or not.

In essence, exhibited by President Obama's own brand of emotionally-charged rhetoric (i.e. emphasizing that illegal immigrants are not "felons" but "families;" not "criminals" but "children"), he too has chosen to accentuate and sympathize with the notion of the United Nations that crossing an international border unbeknownst or without the permission of the violated country is not an illegal act. **And based upon President Obama's actions as well, note the timeliness of his November 2014 announcement of his Executive Order on effectively granting amnesty to 4-5 million illegal immigrants followed on the heels of the major United Nations General Assembly report** issued on the plight of immigrants worldwide by U.N. Secretary-General Ban Ki-moon – just months before (in August 2014).

60,000+ Illegal Immigrant Children Flood U.S. Border

During the summer of 2014, tens of thousands of illegal immigrant children arrived at the U.S. southern border from Central America and Mexico – seeking asylum in the United States claiming to be fleeing for their safety from domestic gang and drug violence in their native countries. In most instances, these children were unaccompanied by their parents who had paid as much as $10,000 or more for their safe passage across the U.S.-Mexican border. Of course, once formal asylum is granted to the children by President Obama's Executive Order, eventually the way would be paved (i.e. the door would be wide open) for their parents in their native country (and extended family members) to legally follow them to the United States.

The Obama Administration had feigned to have had no prior knowledge of the uptick in illegal immigrant children that would be crossing the southern U.S./Mexican border by the summer of 2014 as merely a "cover" and an alibi for not having enhanced border patrol security in anticipation of the upsurge. Although, subsequently, it was learned that six months earlier in January 2014, the Obama Administration had already been making public solicitations to government contractors in preparation for the housing of an anticipated large number increase – in the tens of thousands – in illegal immigrants who would be showing up at the U.S.-Mexico border later that year.

For its part, not surprisingly the United Nations also has publically urged the United States to accept these illegal immigrants, granting them "refugee status." Once having attained refugee status in the U.S., they could then apply for asylum allowing them to obtain permanent residence status in this country. However, most of the illegal immigrants entering the United States were from the countries of Honduras, El Salvador and Guatemala, where – instead of fleeing tradition political and/or ethnic violence, which would qualify them for legal entry – they claimed to be escaping from drug and/or gang violence; which statutorily does not (under current U.S. law) qualify them for asylum and permanent residence entry status in the United States. As a consequence:

> The United Nations High Command for Refugees (UNHCR) wants the 30-year U.N. policy for granting refugee status

to be amended to (include) those fleeing native lands due to violence from gangs and drug cartels, in addition to political and ethnic conflicts. *"Unaccompanied children and families who fear for their lives must not be forcibly returned [to their native countries] without access to proper asylum procedures,"* UNHCR official Leslie Velez said in testimony submitted to the House Judiciary Committee."[47]

Further, the UNHCR said that, if the law were amended, almost 60% (of the illegal immigrant children) could qualify for refugee status or political asylum...and many of the children, perhaps as many as 80 percent, immigration lawyers say, could meet the requirements for a Special Immigrant Juvenile (SIJ) visa, which is offered to minors who make it to the United States who are found to "have been abused, abandoned, or neglected – according to the website of the U.S. Citizenship and Immigration Services.'"[48]

And regarding the legal interpretation and foundation for the United Nation's contention that the rights, protection and security of illegal immigrants are paramount to even the National Security interests of nations concerned about terrorism, one need only to examine the U.N. Secretary-General's General Assembly report, dated August 7, 2014. Specifically, key excerpts from this report illustrate a naïve diametric disregard for 1) any National Security and terrorist considerations and 2) the illegality of immigrants crossing international borders without the knowledge or approval of the destination country – summarily dismissing outright the potentially dire National Security and economic ramifications to its citizenry (Note: the nomenclature, "irregular migration" or "irregular situation" appearing in the following U.N. report excerpts specifically refer to the illegal crossing of an international border):

Paragraph 21: The Convention on the Rights of the Child prescribes that *"no child shall be deprived of his or her liberty unlawfully or arbitrarily (Article 37(b))."* The Committee on the Rights of the Child has recommended that *"detention of a child because of their parents' migration status constitutes a Child's Rights violation and contravenes the principle of the best interests of the child...*(Therefore, Nation) States should expeditiously and completely cease the detention of children on the basis of their migration status.

Commentary: Under current U.S. Immigration administrative and judicial procedure law, the practical effect is that the child will ultimately be released into the United States and given an Immigration hearing date scheduled for months later at which time typically 60%-90% will never show. Secondly, specifically regarding illegal immigrant children, the sentiment of President Obama's Executive Order on Illegal Amnesty is in 100% lockstep compliance with Paragraph 21 of the United Nations proclamation.

Human Rights at the International Border

Paragraph 56: International migration, in particular, irregular migration, is described by some States as a threat to National Security (A/HRC/20/24, para. 8). *States therefore give primacy to security concerns and to preventing the arrival of migrants at international borders. The Special Rapporteur on the human rights of migrants has pointed out that this perspective is at odds with a human-rights-based approach* that sees migrants first and foremost as human beings and as holders of rights rather than a security threat. (A/HRC/23/46, para. 31).

Commentary: Makes one wonder if this specific United Nations paragraph edict is at the heart of President Obama's reluctance, throughout his Presidency, to truly want to close the Southern border, in addition to any ancillary desire on his part to placate U.N. Secretary-General Ban Ki-moon in particular.

> Paragraph 57: Prompted solely by considerations of National Security, border governance without human rights safeguards can lead to human rights violations and a breach of international principles such as non-refoulement [i.e. forcibly returning a refugee to his or her native country]…*Some States mistakenly consider border areas as international zones or excised territory (such as airports, land entry points and islands off the coast of the mainland), where they can act as though they were not bound by legal regimes or their human rights obligations.*

Commentary: Per the United Nations, in essence, International Immigration law supersedes United States Immigration law.

> Paragraph 59: …*[T]he crossing of a national border in an unauthorized manner or overstaying a permit of stay does not constitute a crime. Irregular entry and stay is not properly defined as a crime against persons or property, nor against National Security…*The Working Group on Arbitrary Detention has also stated that "immigrants in irregular situations should not be qualified or treated as criminal or be viewed only from the perspective of National Security (A/HRC/10/21, para. 68)."

Commentary: **According to the United Nations, the act of illegally crossing the border *is not* a crime; or in the case of Barack Obama and many Democrats, not a "real" or serious crime.**

Indeed, the Obama Administration, by its enforcement conduct (or lack thereof), is sanctioning the International Immigration law edict of the United Nations that it is, effectively, *not a crime* to cross an international border unbeknownst or without permission of the destination country.

It must be noted that, since 1986, the Republican Party has occupied the White House 15 of the last 30 years – or half the time. Consequently, the immigration problem, its causes and blame must be equally shared by both Democrats and Republicans. However, echoing the sentiments of law professor Jonathan Turley, according to David Inserra, a research associate of Homeland Security and Cybersecurity at *The Heritage Foundation,* it is not within the authority of President Obama, in particular, to effectively amend a law, ignore the law or through "prosecutorial discretion," exempt whole segments of lawbreakers, especially if based on political or policy considerations.

Accordingly, the following are just two more instances illustrating exactly how the Obama Administration A) has skirted enforcement of U.S. Immigration law during the Obama Presidency in favor of the United Nations' endorsement of International Immigration Law and B) effectively placated and complied with Paragraph 59 of the U.N. Secretary-General's General Assembly report, dated August 7, 2014:

1. In late 2012, the Director of ICE, John T. Morton issued a directive to all ICE enforcement agents "to no longer detain unlawful immigrants if their only offense was being in the country illegally" and

2. In November 2011, the U.S. Citizenship and Immigration

Services agency endorsed ICE's policy of prosecutorial discretion; advising it would stop issuing Notices to Appear before an Immigration judge to illegals who do not meet minimum arbitrarily –set ICE enforcement priorities (like ICE Director Morton's directive noted above).

To accentuate his contention, Inserra quotes the following analogy of John Yoo, a legal official in the George W. Bush Administration:

"Imagine the precedent this claim [of prosecutorial discretion by Obama] would create: President Romney [or, for example, any future President] could lower tax rates simply by saying he will not use enforcement resources to prosecute anyone who refuses to pay capital-gains tax. He could repeal Obamacare simply by refusing to fine or prosecute anyone who violates it."[49]

Further, Paragraph 60: Increased border surveillance and securitization, together with a drastic reduction of avenues for legal migration, force migrants to seek alternatives. To enter destination countries, they are often compelled to travel routes using unsafe means of transport and relying on smugglers; sometimes, they fall prey to traffickers. Consequently, they are susceptible to human rights abuses and violations, including exploitation, trafficking, ill-treatment and sexual violence.

Commentary: Another more likely plausible explanation and motive, in his mind, as to why President Obama has been reluctant to proactively pursue tightening U.S. border security throughout his Presidency.

Human Rights Challenges

> Paragraph 68: Interception practices, where groups of migrants are pushed back to countries of origin or transit, can be arbitrary and lead to human rights violations, including of the principle of non-refoulement. Such practices fail to address the protection needs of migrants [and] put their lives at risk…

Commentary: Again, just another probable explanation and motive as to why President Obama has been reluctant to do more to tighten U.S. border security throughout his Presidency.

What Would the American People Think

If generally known to the public, the above excerpts from the United Nations Secretary-General's August 2014 report as to the primacy of International Immigration law over United States Immigration law would, no doubt, (based on recently Gallup and other polling data) literally stun the collective conscience of the vast majority of American People; meeting with their overwhelming disapproval. Yet upon a reading of these excerpts from the U.N. report, it would alternatively totally explain the tepid, at best, U.S. border security enforcement efforts (and obvious lack of enthusiasm to upgrade them) exhibited by Barack Obama and his Administration during the first seven years of his Presidency.

In so doing, Barack Obama's actions as President have been demonstratively more reflective of his conscious adherence to the guidelines of the United Nations-endorsed International Immigration law; thus effectively serving to elevating it above United States Immigration law. **As a consequence, Mr. Obama – as does the United Nations**

– disregards what a vast majority of American People believe is a serious risk to this country's National Security.

Summarizing, specifically regarding the concerns of Nation States as to National Security and terrorism, according to the U.N. report, *"The Special Rapporteur on the human rights of migrants has pointed out that this [National Security] perspective is at odds with a human-rights-based approach..." para. 56).* Second, strengthening the Southern border of the United States, through *"increased border surveillance and securitization, together with a drastic reduction of avenues for legal migration [would] force migrants to seek [unsafe] alternatives" (para. 68).* Third, specifically, *Interception practices, where groups of migrants are pushed back to countries of origin or transit, can be arbitrary and lead to human rights violations..."* (para. 60).

During his first seven years as President, Mr. Obama, only grudgingly, if at all, gave relatively little consideration to enforcing U.S. Immigration law wherein it contradicted and conflicted with International Immigration law policy and precepts, as specifically reflected in the U.N. report excerpts that are highlighted herein. As a consequence, very few if anyone outside the Obama Administration or in the Democrat Party would objectively dare to describe U.S. Southern border security efforts undertaken by the Obama Administration during the last seven years as robust, in any way, with respect to the enforcement of U.S. Immigration law.

Lastly, Conservatives and Republicans would be wise to, at least, consider more than just Democrat political considerations (i.e. meant to ultimately generate and expand upon a future permanent underclass of new and dependent Democrat voters) as the only motive of Barack Obama in failing to secure the Southern border. To ignore any other possible motive is to limit consideration to only Mr. Obama's time while he is the President of the United States. However, there are more than just Democrat votes at stake here.

Alternatively, one must expand their paradigm of thought and consider the time period beyond 2016, to include the very real possibility that, after leaving office, Barack Obama is also motivated by the political legacy ambition and option of possibly becoming the Secretary-General of the United Nations at some point in the future. **Indeed, virtually everything President Obama has done or proposed to do in the name of U.S. Immigration policy throughout his Presidency has instead been even more consistent and in concert with United Nations-endorsed International Immigration law – thus superseding U.S. Immigration law to which, as President of the United States is Mr. Obama's sworn paramount responsibility.**

CHAPTER 5

38 *National Public Radio* "Obama Goes It Alone, Shielding Up to 5 Million immigrants from Deportation" by Eyder Peralta – November 20, 2014.

39 1) *Judicial Watch* "New Documents Show Homeland Security Released 165,900 Convicted Aliens Throughout U.S." – March 23, 2015. 2) *CNSNews* "ICE: 165,527 Criminal Aliens Loose in U.S.A." by Brittany Hughes – March 19, 2015.

40 *US News* "Republicans Want to Expedite Deportation of Minors" by Lauren Fox – July 9, 2014.

41 *Newsmax* "Barack Obama Immigration Scandal: 11 Key Quotes from the Executive Action Amnesty Controversy" and "8 Key Figures Caught Up in the Executive Action Amnesty" by Alana Marie Burke – January 30, 2015.

42 *Judicial Watch – A Special Campaign Report* - "An Examination of the Obama Administration's Unprecedented and Radical Attempts to Expand Executive Power" – Page 13.

43 *Los Angeles Times* "The President's Power Grab: Obama is Not a Dictator, But There is a Danger in his Aggregation of Executive Power" (Commentary) by Jonathan Turley – March 9, 2014.

44 *Newsmax* – Ibid - January 30, 2015.

45 *Daily Caller* "Fox Poll Reveals Hidden Opposition to Obama's Amnesty" by Neil Munro – December 11, 2014.

46 *Gallup* – Trends: Immigration.

47 *CBSDC* "UN Urges United States to Designate Immigrants as Refugees" (Copyright Associated Press) – July 8, 2014.

48 *FoxNews* "Despite White House Claims, Up to 80% of Migrant Children Can Legally Stay in Country" by Elizabeth Liorente – June 27, 2014.

49 *The Heritage Foundation* "Ten-Step Checklist for Revitalizing America's Immigration System: How the Administration can Fulfill Its Responsibilities" by David Inserra – November 3, 2014.

The United Nations' Anti-Torture Edict to Close Guantanamo Bay

1. *"Furthermore, America – in fact, no nation – can insist that others follow 'the rules of the road' if we refuse to follow them ourselves. For when we don't, our actions appear arbitrary and undercut the legitimacy of future interventions, no matter how justified...When force is necessary, we have a moral and strategic interest in binding ourselves to certain rules of conduct...that is the source of our strength. **That is why I prohibit torture. That is why I order Guantanamo closed."***
   President Barack Obama – Nobel Peace Prize Acceptance Speech – December 10, 2009.

2. ***"It makes no sense to spend $3 million per prisoner to keep open a prison that the world condemns and terrorists use to recruit.** Since I've been President, we've worked responsibly to cut the population of Guantanamo in half. **Now is the time to finish the job. And I will not relent in my determination to shut it down.** It is not who we are."***
   President Barack Obama – State of the Union Address – January 20, 2015

3. During his 2008 Presidential Campaign, although never specifically linking the word "Torture" and Guantanamo Bay in the same sentence, Barack Obama repeatedly referred to the terrorist detainee prison facility as *"a sad chapter in American history."*

By Executive Order, President Obama is determined to close the terrorist detainee prison facility at Guantanamo Bay, Cuba – reassigning what prisoners he cannot pardon before then to the maximum security "Super-Max" prison facility in Colorado and elsewhere in the United States. For political reasons, it may not formally occur until after the 2016 Presidential Election, during the last two and-a-half months of his Presidency. Although, it may have to occur prior to then as the logistical transfer must be complete before he leaves office on January 20, 2017.

What If GTMO Doesn't Close

"I can't say with certainty that we're going to get there [close GTMO], but I can tell you we're going to die trying."
Susan Rice, National Security Advisor – November 4, 2015

The closing of GTMO is problematic if Barack Obama does, indeed, have designs of one day becoming the United Nations Secretary-General. There is no doubt that - whether GTMO is closed down or not before he leaves office - at the very minimum, President Obama must never be perceived as "relenting" in doing everything possible within his power "to shut it down" (or "die trying") - for precisely the following reasons as culled from speeches of high-ranking United Nations officials:

1. *"It is now 10 years since the U.S. government opened the prison at Guantanamo, and now three years since January 2009, when the President [Obama] ordered its closing within 12 months...Yet the facility continues to exist and individuals remain arbitrarily detained – indefinitely – in clear breach of international law."*
Navi Pillay, United Nations High Commissioner for Human Rights – January 23, 2012

2. *"That is why human rights and the rule of law are such important objectives for all who truly care about global security and prosperity. Historically, Americans have understood this country to be in the vanguard of the global human rights movement... true to its own principles, including the struggle against terrorism.* ***[But] Many people are troubled by and confused when the United States appears to abandon the ideals and objectives, and the international instruments [i.e. the United Nations] with which it has long been identified."***
Kofi Annan, then-U.N. Secretary-General – Farewell Speech – December 11, 2006

3. *"The release of the torture report by the U.S. Senate shows that torture is still taking place in many parts of the world, around the world...As I have often said, the prohibition of torture is an absolute principle. There are no situations where it should be used, under any circumstances...Now as this report has been released, this should be the start of a discussion on how the international community can completely stamp out this torture practice."*
Ban Ki-moon, U.N. Secretary-General – U.N. Press Conference – December 17, 2014

Although, at the time of its release in December 2014, there was much criticism from Republicans and Conservatives as to the hurried necessity of a lame-duck, Democrat-controlled U.S. Senate Intelligence Committee to complete the so-called torture report (no doubt with President Obama's urging and blessing); as the Republican Party was poised to take control of Congress and this Committee the following month after having won control of the U.S. Senate in the 2014 Mid-Term elections a month earlier.

Indeed, Republicans staunchly believed that the investigation upon which the Democrat-controlled Senate Committee's conclusions were drawn was decidedly one-sided and, thus, distorted and incomplete. Nevertheless, in effect, the Democrat-controlled Senate Committee report served as a "mea culpa" admission to the world that the "enhanced interrogation techniques" employed by the United States during the War on Terror under the Bush Administration, in fact, constituted torture and were in violation of human rights. **Not surprisingly, the conclusions drawn in the Democrat-controlled Senate Committee's report are in virtual lockstep with all previous condemnation edicts issued since 2006 by the United Nations and its leaders on the subject of torture as it relates to Guantanamo Bay.**

The Subterfuge of GTMO as a "Recruiting Tool"

Regarding President Obama's long-held rationale that GTMO is a recruiting tool for terrorists worldwide, Charles Krauthammer, - arguably one of the most prominent Conservative political thinkers of today - labeled the basis upon which President Obama relies in his "promise" to close the Guantanamo Bay prison facility as being *"irrelevant, it's anachronistic, it's obsolete:"*

"[The American People] are hostages to a promise Obama made [to close Gitmo]. He made a promise to withdraw from Iraq and we saw how that one turned out...Obama has a fixed idea. And this idea is sort of a personal commitment that he made to empty Guantanamo. Why?"
Charles Krauthammer – Political Commentator - *Fox News* – *"Special Report"* – June 5, 2015

More to the point: To whom is Barack Obama primarily concerned about in closing the prison at Guantanamo Bay: The only 1 in 3 American People who want to see GTMO closed or the United Nations – which, since at least 2006, has unequivocally called for the closing of the Guantanamo Bay prison facility, labelling it as a violation of international human rights law? And why?

Per the United Nations Commission on Human Rights Report dated February 15, 2006 (which then-U.N. Secretary-General Kofi Annan endorsed the following day):

> The War on Terror, as such, *does not constitute an armed conflict* for the purposes of the application of international humanitarian law...The interrogation techniques authorized by the (United States) Department of Defense amount to degrading treatment...The United States government should either expeditiously bring all Guantanamo Bay detainees to trial or release them without delay...The United States government should close the Guantanamo Bay detention facilities without delay.[50]

Respectfully, Dr. Charles Krauthammer's assessment of Mr. Obama's long-held contention behind his "recruiting tool" rationale (or pretext) for closing GTMO is based solely within the paradigm of "what is in the best National Security interest of the United States." And if this U.S. National Security best interest paradigm of thought were the sole consideration of Barack Obama, Dr. Krauthammer's assessment is obviously correct. But, as Dr. Krauthammer wondered out loud, "Why?"

It is just as plausible, if not more so that Barack Obama's paradigm of thought criteria driving his fervent insistence that GTMO be closed down appears to 1) rely upon more than just U.S. National Security interests (i.e. a Jihadi recruitment tool) and 2) his future beyond 2016. If alternatively, President Obama believes, in his mind, that the authority of the United Nations – in its 2006 judgment that the United States is in violation of international human rights law by failing to close GTMO – supersedes the concerns of a vast majority of the American People about their own National Security, one can now clearly understand (but, by no means, agree with) Barack Obama's rationale for closing GTMO. And, if true, President Obama's long-stated primary justification for closing Guantanamo – that the prison facility is a terrorist "recruiting tool" worldwide – is then pure subterfuge.

Rather, President Obama wanting to close GTMO because he believes it to be a recruiting tool for terrorists worldwide is 1) ancillary, at best, and 2) no more of an incremental threat to U.S. National Security than, perhaps by comparison, the recruiting tool for terrorists of, alternatively, a perceived weak-kneed image posed by the President of the United States as exemplified by Mr. Obama's half-hearted military response and commitment thus far to actually winning the War against ISIS. **Moreover, if GTMO were closed tomorrow, President Obama cannot possibly be saying that the prison's existence is by any means a tipping point. And, therefore by its closing that**

the terrorist threat would thereafter discernably diminish or just simply melt away.

Candidly, President Obama has made it clear to the world that, in siding with the 2006 U.N. Anti-Torture Edict, Guantanamo should be closed. In particular, Mr. Obama emphatically agrees that, by its existence, the prison serves to suggest the continued use of torture by the United States in violation of international law. But, please drop the pretext that 1) Mr. Obama's primary concern is that the prison poses –as a recruiting tool – a substantial threat to National Security and 2) Mr. Obama is for once, suddenly concern about spending Taxpayer dollars that the government does not have and the $3 million per year it costs per terrorist detainee to house them. And if President Obama is truly concerned about Taxpayer dollars, what about the $600+ million that the Pentagon says is the actual cost it would take to close GTMO and transfer GTMO terrorist detainees to U.S. prisons?

Specifically regarding then-United Nations Secretary-General Kofi Annan's 2006 admonition that *"the United States government should either expeditiously bring all Guantanamo Bay detainees to trial or release them without delay:"* The emphatic immediacy of the U.N. Secretary-General's 2006 statement would also serve to explain 1) President Obama's predilection for downplaying at every turn incidents that are perceived by the American People as obviously ter-ror-related (e.g. The so-called Fort Hood shootings in November 2009, the "Underwear Bomber" over Detroit a month later, etc.) and, thus 2) further exemplify Mr. Obama's determination not to allow the terrorist detainee population at GTMO to grow; at a time when he is relentless-ly trying to reduce it   using whatever pretext he can ‑ to a minimum level that would ultimately justify, in his mind, closing it down.

The American People Decide Otherwise - Not Wanting GTMO Closed or an End to "Harsh Interrogation Techniques" in Extreme Situations:

> **The Senate report (on so-called Torture) on the CIA's harsh interrogation techniques during the George W. Bush Administration comes at a time when America's support for such techniques is at a high point.** Charles Dunlap Jr., a warfare strategy expert and Duke University School of Law Professor, added: *"Don't be surprised if the next poll shows that a sizable percentage of the American public would still support harsh interrogation techniques, short of anything causing permanent physical injury, in an extreme situation, or especially in the aftermath of a serious terrorist attack by ISIS or al-Qaida."*[51]

It bears remembering that, in 2009 – with Democrats controlling both houses of Congress and a Democrat President with approval ratings hovering around 60% - even President Obama couldn't prevail upon Nancy Pelosi, the House Speaker or Harry Reid, the Senate Majority Leader, to pass legislation permitting Mr. Obama to close Guantanamo down; due specifically to public opinion polls of the American People who overwhelmingly wanted the terrorist prison facility to remain open. Even today, the American public has moved little on their adamant preference that GTMO remain open. According to *Gallup Polling*:

> The President appears to be fighting an uphill battle when it comes to Americans' views on closing Guantanamo Bay. Gallup has asked Americans about the Guantanamo Bay prison four times since 2007, prefacing the question by informing respondents that the prison holds "people from other countries who are suspected of being terrorists" and asking

if the prison should or should not be closed and move "some of the prisoners to U.S. prisons." A majority has opposed closing the prison each time Gallup has asked the question. **Most recently, a June 5-8, 2014 Gallup survey showed 66% opposed and only 29% favored closing the prison.**[52]

Likewise, a 2013 Associated Press Poll revealed that a majority of Americans "Strongly or Moderately favored" the use of "harsh interrogation techniques" (so-called torture by the United Nations and President Obama): **51% to 38%**. Moreover, if one includes respondents who were only "Moderately opposed" to the use of harsh interrogation techniques (presumably meaning not opposed in all circumstances), the percent in favor of using harsh interrogation techniques at least under some extreme ("Jack Bauer"-like) circumstances rises to **77% in favor to only 16%** who "Strongly Oppose" the practice in all circumstances (a ratio of 4 to 1 who would approve the use). Although according to Barack Obama's insistence that *"the world condemns"* (i.e. meaning the United Nations condemns) the Guantanamo Bay prison facility, a substantial majority of the American People nevertheless are conversely adamant that it is necessary for it to remain open – whether or not Barack Obama cares to listen to them.

The Obama Drone Policy

> *"This government [The Obama Administration] has decided that – instead of detaining members of Al-Qaeda [at the Guantanamo Bay prison] - they are going to kill them [with Drones]."*

John Bellinger, former Bush Administration Legal Advisor to the State Department and National Security Council, who was responsible for drafting the legal justification for the original Drone Warfare Targeting Policy – May 1, 2013

John Bellinger, speaking before the bi-partisan *Policy Center*, stated his belief that the dramatic increase in Drone Strikes under the Obama Administration was primarily because President Obama *"was unwilling to deal with the consequences of jailing [additional] suspected Al-Qaeda members – [that the] "U.S. would rather kill suspects than send them to [Guantanamo Bay]".* [53]

Does President Obama's Drone Policy, indeed, play a collateral, yet integral function in his ongoing struggle to ultimately close down the Guantanamo Bay terrorist prison facility before he leaves office? When President Obama took office in 2009, Conservatives were surprised, but pleased, that he had chosen not only to continue President George W. Bush's tactical Drone warfare strategy in prosecuting the War on Terror in Pakistan and elsewhere, but to even go beyond – accelerating their use.

Whereas Liberal supporters of President Barack Obama were alternately dismayed but, for the most part, quietly so. For them, Mr. Obama's Drone Policy seemed utterly incongruous given the risk of collateral damage - i.e. the inevitable deaths and injuries to innocent civilians over time – no matter to what extraordinary lengths the CIA and U.S. military went to avoid such unintended consequences.

> *"U.S. drone attacks in Afghanistan, Pakistan and other countries may be militarily effective, but they are killing innocent civilians in a war that is obscene and immoral. I'm afraid that ignoring this ugly fact makes America complicit in murder...Efficacy is not legitimacy, and I don't see how drone strikes can be considered a wholly legitimate way to wage warfare."*
>
> Eugene Robinson, Pulitzer Prize-winning liberal *Washington Post* News columnist – December 2, 2013.

In 2009, President Obama criticized the use of "harsh interrogation techniques" against known terrorist detainees - yet was evidently prepared to readily accept the killing of suspected terrorists and the inevitable collateral drone strike killings of innocent civilians:

> And (in 2009) how does President Obama and the Left accept and reconcile the inconsistency of their endorsement of drone attacks against Al Qaeda - where they, in effect, are also sanctioning the inevitable collateral deaths of innocent civilians? Yet Mr. Obama and his Party stridently insist, as being even more abhorrent, the thought of imparting trust to the arbitrary decision-making authority of even their own duly-elected President to dare "water board" an enemy combatant (which has absolutely no lasting physical or mental effect) who may have knowledge or intelligence of future attacks that could result in the deaths of Americans for - incidentally - a nation still at war.[54]

Although, collaterally, by predominately relying upon Drone strikes as his military tactic of choice in weeding out Al Qaeda from their nests in Pakistan and Afghanistan, President Obama was, indeed knowingly or unknowingly, simultaneously insuring that there would be virtually no additional live-body Islamic terrorists captured "on his watch" with nowhere to house them long-term but the Guantanamo Bay prison facility. Although further compounding the problem for Barack Obama, however, to his surprise in early 2009 the newly-elect President found out that the closing of GTMO would be a formidable challenge – given not only the opposition of the American People, but his own Democrat-controlled Congress as well.

Certainly, the last thing Barack Obama wanted to do was exacerbate this monumental struggle to close GTMO by *increasing*

the number of GTMO detainees. Whereas, aside from the professed morality of Democrats concerned for the collateral deaths of innocents, the reliance on Drone attacks would, concurrently, also turn out to be the most effaceable method for Mr. Obama to prevent the GTMO terrorist detainee population from growing - at a time that Barack Obama was feverishly reducing the number of detainees to so few that it would, in his mind, justify GTMO's permanent closing before he left office. Again, morality aside, is Barack Obama capable of such a Machiavellian thought process as this? Or is this just another mere coincidence.

"The (Obama) White House has overseen an exponential expansion of America's drone war. While President Bush launched fifty-one such strikes, President Obama has presided over 330, according to the London-based Bureau of Investigative Journalism."[55] **Although ultimately in May of 2013, the Obama Administration did reverse course,** implementing a decidedly more stringent agency-coordinated (i.e. CIA and Defense Department) drone strike-targeting policy, designed to essentially eliminate the possibility with "near certainty" of collateral deaths of innocent civilians.

However, as a consequence, the new, more stringent criteria have since severely hampered the U.S. military - curtailing the number and frequency of authorized targeted attacks in Iraq against ISIS since that time. Moreover, due to concerns of the Obama Administration that the CIA, at times, may have been too aggressive in conducting its drone strikes, President Obama (in January 2013) nominated his then-National Security Advisor John Brennan as CIA Director to assume hands-on control of implementing and overseeing the new, more rigid drone strike-targeting policy going forward.

Commenting on the new, more stringent Drone Policy target

criteria introduced in May 2013, President Obama stressed that *"before any [drone] strike is taken, there must be 'near-certain-ty' that no civilians are killed or injured."*[56] By contrast, even the most recent opinion poll revealed a clear majority of 71% of the American People supported the use of drone strikes in the war against ISIS (versus only 22% against), seeing no reason to curtail them.[57]

Specifically from a practical and logistical perspective, the protocol for authorizing and approving drone strikes has now been elevated and centralized offsite in the CIA and military agency high command centers. However, this elevated new command protocol has resulted in prolonged time delays between the time a remote drone operator (or on-site fighter pilot in the case of the current War against ISIS in Iraq) can proceed; typically taking 45 minutes to an hour before final approval to launch an attack is given. The practical effect is to relieve the remote drone operator or on-site pilot of the final respon-sibility (i.e. take out of his/her hands) for the evaluation authority to execute a targeted strike – having elevating that responsibility up the chain of command.

Although, as a consequence, even when authorization is ultimately granted, the optimal target sighting criteria upon which the initial request was made most times had already passed; changing to a "no shoot" situation precisely due to this extended delay of time in granting or denying authorization. Indeed, in 2015, Senator John McCain criticized the Obama Administration noting that 75% of fighter bomber sortie missions over Iraq were returning to base without even dropping their payload due to either 1) the more strin-gent targeting criteria or 2) the extended time-delayed authorization process – or both.

The incidence of innocent civilian deaths from U.S. drone strikes had previously been curtailed from a ratio of 1 in 5 in 2009 to just 1 in 20 by 2012, according to CIA statistical analysis. The decrease in innocent civilian casualties can be further explained by a reassessment (i.e. switch) of targeting preferences. In particular, this dramatic decrease in innocent civilian deaths was also attributed to the fact that, before August of 2010, CIA drone strike-targeting was two-thirds concentrated on the targeting of residences harboring combatants - where there was a more likelihood of innocents and family members being present.

After that time, U.S. drone strikes have concentrated predominantly more on moving vehicles; resulting in a markedly smaller ratio of innocents to enemy combatant deaths. As a consequence, until the accidental collateral killing of two hostages in Pakistan in January 2015, there had been no reports of innocent civilians having been killed by U.S. drone attacks since the new constricted drone strike-targeting policy was implemented nearly two years earlier.[58]

What Really Drove Obama to Curtail Drone Strike-Targeting Even Further

But what specifically changed in the spring of 2013 to have caused President Obama to announce a formal agency-wide change of the U.S. strike-targeting policy and adopt exceedingly more stringent criteria – meant to eliminate, with "near certainty," civilian casualties before authorizing future targeted strikes? Second, regarding the timing of the announcement by President Obama and in keeping with the thesis and analysis of this book, did anything change in the formal stated position and current thinking of the United Nations – in the spring of 2013 with respect to U.S. drone attacks no longer being considered as an acceptable tactical military strategy - that caused President Obama to then abruptly constrict U.S. strike-targeting policy?

Initially, in 2010, CIA drone strikes were ramped up after the devastating Taliban-infiltrated ambush suicide attack on CIA officers, killing seven, during a meeting with a key allied informant (that had recently joined the Taliban) who detonated a suicide bomb. Further, prior to 2012, it should be noted that, under the leadership of then-Defense Secretary Leon Panetta, a more aggressive drone strike posture was adopted and approved by the White House; accounting for the substantial increase in drones strikes under President Obama. Indeed, drone strikes increased more than six fold under President Obama in just four years as opposed to under President George W. Bush i.e. 330 to 51.

Obama Reflexively Reacts to U.N. Charges of U.S. Violating International Law with Drone Strikes

As previously stated, in May 2013, President Obama made his formal announcement of a revised U.S. drone strike-targeting policy meant to virtually eliminate the possibility of future civilian deaths, in remarks made at the National Defense University in Washington DC. However, specifically coinciding with the timing of President Obama's announcement - just two months earlier in March 2013 - United Nations Special Envoy on Human Rights and Counter-Terrorism, Ben Emmerson had publically declared the United States to be in violation of international human law regarding U.S. drone strikes.[59]

Previously (and perhaps surprisingly to many), regarding the United Nations' standing position on the use of drone attacks as an acceptable military tactic:

[Emmerson] "acknowledged that *'if used in strict*

compliance with the principles of International Human Law, remotely-piloted aircraft are capable of reducing the risks of civilian casualties in armed conflict.'" Beyond that statement, Emmerson additionally noted that currently "there is *'no clear international consensus'* on laws controlling the deployment of drone strikes. (Although,) while the fact that civilians have been killed or injured does not necessarily point to a violation of international human law, it undoubtedly raises issues of accountability and transparency (in which Emmerson specifically cited the CIA for criticism)."[60]

In particular, based upon his March 2013 U.N. Special Envoy fact-finding trip to Pakistan, Emmerson seized upon the prerequisite that a nation launching a drone attack must have the prior consent of the sovereign nation in which the drone attack occurs; which led Emmerson to conclude that the United States had, thus violated international human law. To wit, according to his investigation, Emmerson stated that Pakistan *"considers it to be a violation of [its] sovereignty and territorial integrity;"* claiming it had not given the United States permission to conduct certain drone strikes; a charge which the U.S. vigorously disputed.[61]

What followed two months later (May 23, 2013 at the National Defense University) with regard to his new restricted U.S. drone strike-targeting policy, President Obama stated the following bullet points as if a direct answer, reassurance and remedy to U.N. Envoy Emmerson's specific concerns:

1. *"Beyond the Afghan theater, we only target Al-Qaeda and its associated forces. And even then, the use of drones is heavily constrained."*

2. *"America does not take strikes when we have the ability to capture individual terrorists. Our preference is always to detain, interrogate and prosecute."*

3. *"America cannot take drone strikes whenever we choose. Our actions are bound by consultation with partners and respect for State sovereignty."*

4. Regarding President Obama's case for using drone strikes: *"Conventional airpower or missiles are not as precise as drones and are likely to cause more civilian casualties and more local outrage...But by narrowly targeting our action, against those who want to kill us and not the people they hide among, we are choosing the course of action least likely to result in the loss of innocent life."*

Obama acolytes may counter that, even prior to U.N. Envoy Emmerson's March 2013 charge, President Obama – six months earlier in September of 2012 – had already ordered his then-National Security Advisor John Brennan to initiate his own evaluation as to whether the criteria for drone strike-targeting was being abused by the CIA. In fact, at about the same time, the CIA was lobbying to extend and intensify its drone strike warfare in Yemen and other North African nations.[62] Secondly, those cynics might argue further that, in January 2013 (and two months before Emmerson's March 2013 charge), President Obama had already nominated Brennan to take over as permanent CIA Director, to personally monitor on site and rein in future CIA drone strike-targeting policy. All of which is true if only considered in a vacuum.

Except, unless merely another coincidence, it should be noted that *prior to* President Obama's September 2012 initial order to Brennan to begin reviewing the CIA drone attack and targeting policy, in August 2012 – just one month earlier - U.N. Envoy Emmerson first began publically lobbying against the United States - calling for it to voluntarily turn over video tapes of all U.S. drone attacks for United Nations review.

Consequently, if President Obama had not already received a private "heads up" from his upper echelon contacts at the United Nations before, he certainly got the message by August 2012 with Emmerson's publicized recommendation that the United States hand over video of all U.S. drone attacks. Moreover, ultimately just two months later in October 2012, Emmerson, appearing at Harvard University, formally announced that the United Nations was impaneling a special investigations unit to examine "claims of civilian deaths in individual U.S. drone strikes."

Further, it should be noted that both Russia and China – as permanent members of the Security Council (and, incidentally, having veto power over future U.N. Secretary-General Nominations) – had publically endorsed the action taken by the United Nations to initiate such an investigation.[63] As a consequence, it is indeed plausible that an accommodation to severely restrict U.S. drone strike-targeting policy in the future would be made by the Obama Administration and, in fact ultimately was in May 2013.

Conclusion

1. Obama's Preference to Kill Rather than Capture Terrorists

The charge by former George W. Bush National Security Council Legal Advisor John Bellinger that President Obama, in prosecuting the War on Terror, is consciously driven by a purposeful strategy to kill rather than capture terrorists is a serious one made by a prominent and knowledgeable terrorist expert. Nevertheless, it is an allegation with no observable indication - supported by either statements or specific demonstrated actions – that President Obama's preference for drone strikes as his military tactic of choice in prosecuting the War on Terror is in any way influenced by a conscious intent and desire to kill rather than capture terrorists to avoid increasing the detainee population at the Guantanamo Bay prison facility any further.

It cannot be denied that the ancillary negative military consequence from conducting drone strikes precludes the ability to capture and interrogate terrorists for intelligence gathering purposes. However, during his May 2013 speech at the National Defense University, President Obama not only stated it once, but twice that *"when we have the ability to capture individual terrorists, our preference is always to detain, interrogate and prosecute."* In the absence of any statement or demonstrated action to the contrary, President Obama must be taken at his word.

2. The Timing of Obama's Restrained Drone Targeting Strategy Coincides with U.N. Condemnation

However, exactly how Obama's change in restricting drone targeting policy mirrored, in terms of timing, the United Nations condemnation of the United States is quite a different matter. **Specifically, the timing of President Obama (in May 2013) formally announcing the first major curtailment of his drone targeting strategy in four-plus years occurred only two months after the first open charge against U.S. drone attacks by the United Nations on the subject (in March 2013).**

Until U.N. Envoy Emmerson's declaration against U.S. drone policy in March 2013, President Obama, in effect, had been "in sync" with the United Nations; which, until that time, had no formal objection against the use of drone strikes as a military tactic against enemy combatants – so long as the United States 1) secured the prior consent of the nation in which the attack occurred and that 2) avoiding innocent deaths were deemed a major priority concern in drone strike-targeting authorization. **However reiterating, always mindful of, if not consciously and immediately taking his cue from United Nations policy directives, just two months after Emmerson's declaration of U.S. human rights violations**, in May 2013, President Obama 1) reiterated that future U.S. drone strikes will only occur with the prior approval of the host country and 2) announced the implementation of strict constraints on target approval criteria and protocol under which the CIA and the Defense Department must now operate going forward.

However, as a consequence, both the CIA and military have been severely constrained from optimally prosecuting the War on Terror because of the highly constrictive strike-targeting criteria. Just the 75% of bomber aircraft returning from sorties against ISIS over Iraq without having bombed their prescribed enemy target sites is evidence enough of the diminution in effectiveness of both the CIA and the military in their ability to prosecute the War on Terror.

Which begs the question: Was the timing of President Obama tightening strike-targeting constraints driven primarily by his conscious desire to immediately "fall in line" with changing United Nations policy? And, more specifically, was the implementation of such constraining "near certainty" strike criteria also meant to, at all costs, eliminate virtually any future innocent deaths that may occur before he leaves office which could only invite additional scrutiny and criticism from the United Nations - to the potential detriment of any desire Mr. Obama may have of one day becoming the Secretary-General of the United Nations?

Emblematic of the extreme degree to which President Obama is both wary and adverse to even the possibility of a single collateral death, his revised targeting policy prevented drones and military aircraft from the task of easily taking out Iraqi oil tanker trucks transporting and selling ISIS black market oil before they crossed the border into Turkey - only because of the possibility that the truck drivers might be civilians. Yet, as a consequence of his inaction, until this prohibition was recently lifted (in the fall of 2015), President Obama's restricted bomber targeting policy effectively permitted ISIS to garner at least $500 million dollars in oil revenue over a period of a year and a half to finance the cost of prosecuting and promoting their terror and war atrocities worldwide.

Based on events (i.e. the U.N. charge of U.S. drone policy violations of international human law in March 2013) and President Obama's reaction to them (i.e. the immediate implementation of a new, exceedingly constricted U.S. strike-target policy just two months later), it is clearly evident that Mr. Obama is willing to accept more readily the prospect of a stalemated war with ISIS during the last two years of his Presidency – and the incremental tens of thousands of casualties that will inevitably result.

Ultimately, in a limp, almost absurd attempt to deflect criticism from the President's fear of collateral damage deaths, alternatively, the Obama Administration meekly attempted to justify delaying - for 18 months - the bombing of ISIS oil tanker trucks; stating its apprehension was due to the atmospheric pollution the bombings would cause. However, if true, consider the absurdity that President Obama was willing to allow ISIS to earn hundreds of millions of dollars in black market oil revenue to carry on its worldwide jihad simply because of his distress at the carbon footprint that would be created by bombing ISIS oil tanker trucks in the Iraqi desert - as being a greater National Security threat.

The GTMO Effect of the 2014 Beau Bergdahl Prisoner Swap

Given the resounding rejection by the American People of President Obama's insistence that the Guantanamo Bay prison be closed, many had assumed the idea of closing GTMO to be dead – both politically and legislatively. However, in 2014, an arbitrary Executive Decision strategy emerged wherein President Obama began discernably accelerating the "emptying" of terrorist detainees from GTMO by having them suddenly declared, from a U.S. National Security perspective 1) safe for return and 2) at low risk to actively return to the War on Terror against the United States. And once that number of remaining detainees becomes sufficiently small (e.g. 75-100), it is anticipated that President Obama will use his "excessive cost per detainee" pretext as a further rationale to buttress justification for – through Executive Order - closing down the GTMO prison facility and transferring the remaining terrorist detainees to Federal prison facilities on American soil before leaving office in January 2017.

Although, it should further be noted that President Obama must be aware that, once transferred to prisons on American soil, the terrorist detainees could then petition U.S. Courts, under Habeas Corpus, forcing the Federal Government to either immediately try to convict them in civilian court (a dubious and potential daunting task to prove beyond a reasonable doubt based on Federal civilian court "Rules of Evidence") or release them from prison.

The only problem for President Obama occurred when, in 2014, Secretary of Defense Chuck Hagel began to balk at the release of certain terrorist detainees. Hagel as Defense Secretary was required to "sign off" on the release of terrorist detainees attesting to his belief, from a National Security Threat perspective that they would not return to take active part in ongoing terrorist activities. It was suggested that, over time, Hagel had been losing favor with President Obama for "slow-walking" the GTMO prisoner detainee release process.

By the fall of 2014, (Hagel later confirmed that) White House pressure to pick up the pace of certifying terrorist releases left Hagel no choice but to resign. However, the problem ultimately became no problem at all for President Obama who merely replaced Hagel with someone Mr. Obama anticipated would continue the parade of GTMO terrorist detainee releases regardless – Ash Carter. Indeed, 27 of the 33 terrorists released in 2014 occurred with extreme rapidity - during November and December of the year – following Defense Secretary Hagel's resignation.

Re: The 5 for 1 Swap of Bergdahl for Talaban Leaders

Naively, President Obama felt that a White House Rose Garden Announcement (with Bergdahl's parents present) coupled with 1) his stated professed obligation to seek the return of any American POW, even if an alleged deserter, as well as 2) White house denials of having ever been made aware by the military of the allegations that Bergdahl had, indeed, defected to the Taliban, would ameliorate any potential blowback to the prisoner swap for an alleged American POW deserter. It didn't. Although, regardless whatever level of blowback, the deal was done and of even more significance to President Obama, in a Machiavellian sense five more GTMO detainees were now gone for which – under any other circumstance – their release would never have occurred.

(However), Army Sgt. Beau Bergdahl walked away from his base in Afghanistan June 30, 2009, and by December of that year, the President's primary military advisor, then-Chairman of the Joint Chiefs Admiral Mike Mullen, knew those details, according to three of Bergdahl's platoon mates.

"If Mullen knew, and now it's alleged that he did know it, it would be unthinkable that he didn't pump it up the chain of command, his chain of command, or tell the President directly," explained Brad Blakeman, who served in the Bush Administration. *"At a minimum, this would have been included in the President's daily [Intelligence] briefing, and at a maximum, it would've been told directly to the President by Mullin."*[64]

Consequently, for the White House to initially attempt to quell criticism of President Obama by putting out the story that Mr. Obama – before making the swap - knew nothing of the seriousness of allegations against Bergdahl leveled by his platoon mates - i.e. that Bergdahl, indeed, had deserted - begs credulity. One is left to wonder whether President Obama would have released even more than the five terrorist detainees if he thought, strategically, he could have politically "weathered" the incremental outrage such a decision on his part would have wrought from both the public and Congress.

To say nothing of President Obama consciously and capriciously dismissing Congress throughout the entire process; as evidenced by his failure to advise Congress of his "deal" 30 days in advance as required by law. Nevertheless, Barack Obama "succeeded" in arbitrarily reducing the terrorist inmate population at Guantanamo Bay by five more than he otherwise could have by orchestrating this one-sided prisoner swap strategy when he did.

꙳꙳꙳

The questions of 1) the United Nations Anti-Torture Edict to Close Guantanamo Bay as well as 2) the 2013 revised curtailment of drone and military strike-targeting policy are just two more of numerous U.S. foreign policy issues noted throughout upon which Barack Obama has reflexively chosen to systematically side with the official consensus of thought as dictated by United Nations Policy. Rather than the U.S. National Security interests as expressed in opinion polls by a sizable majority of the American People, to whom, as their President, Mr. Obama is sworn and owes his primary allegiance.

Ultimately, even if it proves necessary logistically that the GTMO detainee transfer process commence before the 2016 Presidential Election, in Barack Obama's mind, so be it. However if so, in this particular instance, Barack Obama's own potential post-Presidential political ambition to become the U.N. Secretary-General at some point in the future could very well end up contributing to the defeat of the Democrat Party in the 2016 Presidential Election.

CHAPTER 6

50 Report (by) the United Nations Working Group on Arbitrary Detention: "Situation of Detainees at Guantanamo Bay" dated February 15, 2006 – Recommendations and Conclusions: pages 36-38; paragraphs 83, 87, 95 and 96.

51 *FiveThirtyEight* – "Americans Have Grown More Supportive of Torture" by Brittany Lyte – December 9, 2014.

52 *Gallup.com Poll* "Americans' Views on 10 Key State of the Union Proposals" – January 25, 2015.

53 *The Guardian* "US Drone Strikes Being Used as Alternative to Guantanamo" by Dan Roberts – May 2, 2013.

54 *What Obama and the Democrats Knew that McCain Didn't* - Ibid (Copyright 2009) - Page 92.

55 *The Nation* "America's Secret War in 134 Countries" by Nick Turse – January 16, 2014.

56 *The Guardian* "Drone Strikes by US May Violate International Law, Says UN" by Owen Bowcott – October 18, 2013.

57 *Fox News Opinion Poll* – May 31, 2015-June 2, 2015.

58 *The New Yorker* "The Unblinking Stare" by Steve Coll – November 24, 2014.

59 *ABC News* "U.S. Drone Strikes in Pakistan are Illegal, says UN" by Dana Hughes – March 13, 2013.

60 *The Guardian* – Ibid - October 18, 2013.

61 *ABC News* – Ibid – March 13, 2013.

62 Newamerican.com "CIA Wants More Drones to do in N. Africa What Its Done in Pakistan" by Joe Wolverton, II J.D. – 10/26/2012.

63 *The Bureau of Investigative Journalism* "U.N. Team to Investigate Civilian Drone Deaths" – October 25, 2012.

64 *Fox News Politics* "Bergdahl's platoon mates 'Head of Joint Chiefs Knew he Walked Off Base in 2009'" by Catherine Herridge – April 17, 2015.

How Obama's Adherence to U.N. Policy Restricts Him in Dealing with ISIS, Iraq and Syria

As in the first two years of his Presidency, Barack Obama – through word and action – has continued invoking his predilection for the United Nations' geopolitical model of global governance: Multinationalism (i.e. co-equal nations). The converse of which, by definition, is the outright distain and rejection of stronger nations (e.g. the United States) that the United Nations perceives as singularly elevating their own national interests without even considering or seeking the approval of the "community of nations":

> *"More people and governments understand that Multinationalism is the only path in our interdependent and globalizing world. Global problems demand global solutions - and going it alone is not an option."*
> Ban Ki-moon, U.N. Secretary-General – October 24, 2007.

> *"The idea that there is one people in possession of the truth, one answer to the world's ills, or one solution to humanity's needs has done untold harm throughout history – especially in the last century."*
> Kofi Annan then-U.N. Secretary-General – Nobel Prize Acceptance Speech – December 10, 2001

"No nation can make itself secure by seeking supremacy over all others...We can only do these things by working together through a multi-lateral system...In fact, it is only through multi-lateral institutions that [Member] States can hold each other to account."

"It is, of course, the basic principle of democracy that governments should be accountable to those they govern. **But today the actions of one State can often have a decisive effect on the lives of people of other States. So does it not owe some account to those other States and their citizens as well as its own? I believe it does...***I think that gives the people and institutions of such powerful States a special responsibility to take account of global views and interests, as well as national ones, when making decisions."*
Kofi Annan, then-U.N. Secretary-General – U.N. Farewell Address – December 11, 2006

"And I hope that when, next time, one is dealing with a border threat to the international community, one will wait and seek the approval of the [U.N.] Security Council...It's only the Security Council that has the legitimacy to authorize action on that basis."
Kofi Annan then-U.N. Secretary-General – Final U.N. Press Conference – December 19, 2006

Compared to like-statements made by President Barack Obama exemplifying his preference for Multinationalism and the Global Governance philosophy advocated by the United Nations and his intention that the United States also embrace it:

1. **"No world order that elevates one nation or a group of nations over another will succeed."**

2. *"America has acted unilaterally, without regard for the interests of others."*

3. *"But it is my deeply held belief that in the year 2009– more than at any time in human history – the interests of nations and people are shared...The United States stands ready to begin a new chapter of international cooperation – one that recognizes the rights and re-sponsibilities of all nations."*
President Barack Obama – His first speech before the United Nations General Assembly – September 29, 2009

Further, never having been shy about touting whatever he may con-strue as an accomplishment, who better than Barack Obama himself to convey, highlight and insure that the rest of the world - and the U.N. Secretary-General in particular - fully recognize his efforts on behalf of and in reverence for the hallmark Multinational model of geopolitical global governance espoused by the United Nations:

"People don't remember that when I came into office, in world opinion, the United States ranked below China and barely above Russia. And today, once again, the United States is the most respected country on earth. And part of that, I think, is because of the work we did to re-engage the world and say 'we want to work as partners' – with mutual interest and mutual respect. It's on that basis that we were able to end two wars while still focusing on the very real threat of terrorism...(Although) I'd like to add this: It's im-portant for America to realize that it's not perfect either."
President Barack Obama referencing what he believes to be one of his Presidential legacy accomplishments – June 2, 2015

This, in essence, is the self-proclaimed foreign policy doctrine of a "Light Footprint" and the definition of the term "Leading from Behind" that President Obama has invoked and employed throughout his Presidency. However, because of his commitment to Multinational global governance and what he perceives as the necessity for assuaging the concerns of both U.N. Secretaries-General Ban Ki-moon and Kofi Annan, Barack Obama today has left the United States in a state of paralysis in dealing with Radical Islamic Terrorism and, in particular, the current ISIS threat in Iraq, Syria and elsewhere.

Iraq and ISIS Occupation:

"I was elected to end wars, not start them."
President Barack Obama – September 6, 2013

The perceived necessity to 1) rigidly preserve his seminal Presidential legacy promise - i.e. vowing to end two wars and to not start any new ones – combined with 2) his latent interest to one day become the U.N. Secretary-General, when contrasted against the current U.S. National Security imperative to militarily confront and combat the immediate and formidable ISIS threat in the Middle East has left President Obama flummoxed and hamstrung. To be precise, to now re-commit the requisite number of ground troops necessary to root out ISIS from Iraq would, in Barack Obama's mind, render meaningless his previously claimed Presidential legacy success of having "ended" the Iraq War. Especially, as President Obama sees it, if U.S. forces were not able to accomplish "degrading and destroying" ISIS before he was to leave office in January 2017.

However, the *Washington Post* candidly assessed the dilemma currently facing the Obama Administration if it continues to merely "stand pat" in the War against ISIS in Iraq:

> Now in the seventh year of his Presidency, Obama - who first campaigned for the presidency vowing to end involvement in Iraq and Afghanistan – has brought home the bulk of U.S. forces and hailed this Memorial Day (2015) as *the first time in 14 years the U.S. is not engaged in a major ground war.* But American troops remain mired and at risk in both countries.[65]

And why is that? Precisely because of his aloof and indifferent concern about convincing the Iraqi government as to the necessity for leaving a requisite troop presence in Iraq after the war to insure continuity and peace, President Obama understood and equated "ending the war," instead to mean slashing U.S. troop levels as drastically and as expeditiously as possible. Whereas Brit Hume once remarked that military experts likened leaving U.S. forces in Iraq to an insurance policy. Indeed, given his near-absolute distain for all military conflict, the lesson never learn by Barack Obama about the post-World War II era was that leaving a requisite U.S. troop force after a major military conflict ends (perhaps indefinitely if need be) is, in effect, an insurance policy on a long-term investment in international security - as evidenced after World War II in then-West Germany, Japan, the establishment of NATO throughout Europe and later, South Korea.

Nonetheless, President Obama doesn't appear to be getting any pressure from the United Nations to tread lightly in the War against ISIS in Iraq and Syria. Quite the contrary, in September 2014, the U.N. Security Council – not only with the support of Secretary-General Ban Ki-moon but Russia and China as well – voted unanimously passing U.N. Resolution 2170 (2014) "condemning gross, widespread abuse of human rights in both Iraq and Syria by extremist groups." ISIS and the Al-Nusra Front were specifically named as well as all other terrorist groups associated with Al-Qaida. Additionally, the resolution demanded that these extremist groups "cease all violent acts and immediately disarm and disband" and the U.N. resolved that their heinous, murderous acts against innocent civilians constituted crimes against human rights. Further, the United Nations declared that all guilty terrorists must be brought to justice. Consequently, it is not the United Nations that is holding back Barack Obama in prosecuting the War against ISIS.

Finally, even prominent Democrat Senator Diane Feinstein, the ranking member of the U.S. Senate Intelligence Committee, is on record calling for a much stronger military response to ISIS in both Iraq and Syria - advising that President Obama's current ISIS military strategy (November 2015) is simply too timid. *It has become clear that limited air strikes and support for Iraqi forces and the Syrian opposition are not sufficient to protect our country and our allies.*

President Obama's Real ISIS M.O.

"I think that a deeper problem with the President is this: At times of crises, Americans can normally tell you how their President really thinks...I have an eerie sense with ISIS and the President that he is never quite telling us what his thoughts are – and we perceive it. And it leaves us with our head at a tilt...because he's not even telling us what he really thinks."

Peggy Noonan, noted Journalist and former speech writer for President Ronald Reagan (*MSNBC Morning Joe*) - November 24, 2015

However, by militarily introducing tens of thousands of U.S. combat troops into the conflict at this time, President Obama more likely perceives that he A) would not only have failed to keep his promise to truly end the War in Iraq before he left office, but that B) such a military commitment would also run counter to his assiduously nurtured image as a non-confrontational peacemaker on the world stage. Illustratively, remember what happened in 2009, when Obama Administration officials rebuffed European leaders Angela Merkel and Nicolas Sarkozy, who had urged President Obama to boldly confront Iran with evidence obtained of a secret Iranian weapons-grade uranium facility. However (as previously stated), at the time, Obama's political handlers maintained that such a confrontation would have overshadowed and potentially spoiled "the image of success for Mr. Obama's debut at the U.N."

Although, if the political self-interest of 1) preserving Barack Obama's Presidential legacy and 2) his potential desire to become the United Nations Secretary-General someday are allowed to trump the immediate National Security interest of the United States and the American People in degrading and destroying ISIS, then Mr. Obama really has no choice (from solely a political and personal ambition perspective) but to hope that he will be able "to run out the clock" on the ISIS terror threat until the end of his second term - without having to escalate the commitment to the requisite number of U.S. troops necessary to get the job done.

Yet, if true, Mr. Obama is in effect acknowledging that he is prepared to settle for a stalemate if need be as a higher priority to him. Just "keep a lid" on the conflict until the end of his term and then hand off the inevitable ramped-up military resolution of the War against ISIS in Iraq to the next President. Moreover, to do otherwise would ruin his meticulously crafted United Nations resume.

"From the start, our goal has been first to contain, and we have contained them."
President Barack Obama on United States progress thus far in "containing" ISIS – November 13, 2015

(Only hours later, France suffered the most deadly attack on its soil since World War II at the hands of ISIS).

However, it would seem like a longshot for President Obama to think that he could continue at the same meager level of military commitment – i.e. 3,000 U.S. troops and Special Forces on the ground plus air support – until January 2017. Although, in 2008, who would have thought Barack Obama could have strung out the Iranian nuclear weapons development dilemma seven years without resolution – either through a negotiated and "truly verifiable" disarmament or military intervention? But he has.

Obama Administration "Waters Down" Intel on ISIS' Success

But does that mean the Obama Administration is going to just sit there and wring its hands hoping that ISIS remains at bay until President Obama leaves office? Apparently not. In September 2015, *The Daily Beast* (a noted "hard-left" website historically sympathetic to Obama) stunningly reported, in what is being termed as a "revolt" among more than 50 intelligence analysts at the U.S. military's Central Command (CENTCOM), that since October 2014, their intelligence reports were being "inappropriately altered by senior officials." Specifically, in the formal complaint filed on behalf of the analysts, it was alleged that, **on a systematic basis, the conclusions of analysts' reports were being altered or re-written to disguise the fact that ISIS was, in fact, a stronger, more capable military**

threat than CENTCOM and the Obama Administration were publically portraying them to be:

> The (Intelligence) reports were changed by CENTCOM higher-ups to adhere to the (Obama) Administration's public line that the U.S. is winning the battle against ISIS and al Nusra, al Qaeda's branch in Syria, the analysts claimed (on condition of anonymity...Other) reports crafted by the analysts that were too negative in their assessments of the war were sent back the chain of command or not being shared up the chain.[66]

Just as critical, other sources within the intelligence community have revealed that the **specific military strike-targeting recommendations that intelligence analysts typically make were, many times, purposely and inappropriately removed from their reports** before they were passed up the chain of command to CENTCOM, which is responsible for the final authorization of military strikes in Iraq against ISIS.[67] If true, it would, indeed, serve as added corroboration for the contention of many, including Senator John McCain (Chairman of the U.S. Senate Committee on Armed Services), as to the negative consequences of President Obama's May 2013 revision restricting future military strike-targeting criteria. Yet, it would also serve as another "method" (albeit legally questionable and now under investigation by the Pentagon Inspector General) to 1) "filter out" and reduce the number of strike-targeting opportunities for the U.S. military to pursue in the War against ISIS and, consequently 2) further reduce the risk and negative impact of more collateral deaths to innocent civilians during the remainder of President Obama's term in office.

Finally, given her penchant for controlling all White House

operations, it is hard to imagine that Valerie Jarrett played no role nor had any prior knowledge of all this.

But Is the War against ISIS in Iraq Winnable?

The Obama Administration going public in its criticism of the Iraqi army for a "cut and run" attitude was, indeed, warranted - even at the risk of incurring the ire of the Shiite-dominated Iraqi government in Baghdad. Ultimately and empirically, if the people native to a country are not willing to fight for it, in the long-term, their country will perish no matter how powerful the assisting occupying force (i.e. the United States). As the host country, Iraq and its army *must rightly assume the primary responsibility* and serve in combat as "the tip of the spear" in regaining and holding its own territory. Was this not the enduring cardinal (and regrettable) lesson learned in the prosecution of the Vietnam War?

U.S. forces in Iraq – no matter what the requisite number may be - can embed, actively assist and advise on the ground in standing up the Iraqi army. But the forward combat participation and physical battlefield risk of U.S. troops must remain as minimal as possible – remembering it is now, once again, the Iraqis who must ultimately take their country back. And, however many U.S. ground troops are needed to accomplish the task, President Obama must then commit, but not before.

Revealingly, the current dilemma faced by Iraq is analogous to what occurred during the Korean War. In particular, the American and native Korean-led armies fought separately. Prior to that time, the Korean army units were – as in Iraq - trained and led by U.S. troops and performed admirably. However, during the conflict, when the Korean army units took over responsibility for leading their own units, they failed miserably. The cause – not unlike in Iraq today - was attributed to the lack of trained experienced army unit leaders. In the Iraqi army of today, the one primary distinction and down-fall as to the performance of the Iraqi army is that, after American troops left Iraq for good in 2011, the Shiite-dominated government in Bagdad purged the country's American-trained Iraqi army unit leadership – many of whom were Sunnis – replacing them with un-trained Shiite loyalists with virtually no military experience.

Moreover, it is unfathomable as to why our country is not support-ing the Kurds (who have proven that they can defend themselves with minimal U.S. ground participation) by *directly supplying them with war armaments;* rather than insisting upon going through the Shiite-dominated Iraqi government in Bagdad, which refuses to share power and weaponry equitably. Ultimately, in the fight against ISIS and in the long-term, practicably it would optimally prove to be better for the United States to cut its losses and formally drop the unworkable notion of a "United" Iraq. Going forward, this country would be wise to formally commit our support and security protec-tion 1) behind the Kurds in the northern Iraq and 2) re-establish Sunni trust and military control in the Anbar Province; recognizing both groups as two separate and distinct countries. And, realistical-ly concede the security of the Baghdad Shiite government against ISIS and the territory it controls to Shiite Iran. Frankly, the Baghdad Shiite government was officially free to cast its lot with Iran the day the last U.S. troops left Iraq in 2011.

However, above all, Barack Obama cannot and will not countenance such a strategy as a U.S.-backed formal break-up of Iraq before he leaves office - which again would be tantamount to an admission of failure and another hollow Presidential legacy assertion of Barack Obama as a peacemaker on the world stage, having previously claimed to have "ended two wars" during his Presidency. **Although, bluntly, it would be, with all due respect for the office he holds, immoral for a President of the United States to postpone - for more than two years - the resolution of unchecked ISIS aggression (and the incremental tens of thousands of innocent civilians who will die) by waiting to leave it to his successor to militarily mop up if the motivation is nothing more than an overarching, calculated political strategy driven by self-serving Presidential legacy and future (post 2016) ambitions.** And if there is any other plausible explanation or motivation, President Obama is obligated to tell the American People.

Moreover, isn't it ironic that President Obama spent the first four years of his Presidency blaming his predecessor, George W. Bush, for his shortcomings in both economic and foreign policy – successfully getting him past his 2012 re-election. Yet, Mr. Obama somehow feels that he can escape any future criticism or responsibility – be it in foreign affairs or the economy - if he can merely get passed his last day in office.

Candidly, for anyone who may aspire to lead the nations of the world as a United Nations Secretary-General, what about the tens of thousands of people in the Middle East who, most assuredly, will die at the hands of ISIS in the interim two years, if, indeed, it is Barack Obama's cold calculation to "run the clock out" and leave the elimination of ISIS to his successor to resolve militarily. And those tens of thousands of innocents "in the crosshairs" and in refugee camps simply will have no choice but to wait until January 2017 for another U.S. President to assume responsibility.

But, do their tens of thousands of lives not matter as much as, by comparison to (albeit regrettable) the relatively fewer number of inevitable 1) American troops lost and injured and 2) the incremental number of innocent lives that will also be lost in collateral bombing incidents (i.e. the Fog of War) if President Obama were to abandon his "stand pat" military strategy that is now currently handcuffing the military and CIA by inflexibly and significantly limiting bombing and drone strikes and refusing to commit the requisite level of U.S. troops to win now? **Is it not possible that the overriding motivation driving all of this "stand pat" military strategy is about optimally preserving Barack Obama's image as a world peacemaker – thus, qualifying him as worthy of, one day, ascending to the office of U.N. Secretary-General?** Again, if a more plausible explanation or rationale for President Obama's scant, half-hearted military response to the ISIS threat in Iraq to date exists, the American People have yet to hear it.

Obama is Not a Pacifist

In 2007, it is widely believed that Barack Obama's Presidential candidacy received a pivotal and timely boast in Iowa when he spoke, referring to Iraq, that the U.S. military must stay out of "someone else's civil war" in the Middle East. However, having said that, it has put him in a political hole ever since on a promise that appears he cannot now take back if he were to re-arm Iraq in 2015 – with arms and American troops - to the requisite level needed to defeat ISIS. Moreover, it could tarnish and jeopardize his cultivated pristine image around the world as an anti-war world peacemaker. Bluntly, as Bill Schneider, resident scholar at the moderate Democrat think tank *Third Way*, said, the White House "doesn't want to be remembered for starting wars."[68]

But, remember: In 2013 President Obama ultimately had no backing from the United Nations and only three nations of the international community when he adamantly proposed decisive military action - stating that the deaths of innocent civilians at the hands of President Assad and his use of chemical weapons were intolerable, justifying a punitive military strike against Syria. **However, by contrast, unlike his "red line" threat pronouncement to punitively strike Syria, this time against ISIS, President Obama does, indeed, have the unquestioned backing of a United Nations Security Council resolution (including the personal approval of U.N. Secretary-General Ban Ki-moon, the Russians and China), the European Union and Pope Francis as well to do what it will ultimately take to defeat ISIS.**

One Year into the War against ISIS with No Strategy to Win

"I want to understand why...I'm asking about the President: What is the President's motivation in constantly underestimating the [ISIS terror threat]?...It's confounding and I'm still trying to figure out what's behind it. Why are they saying these things that they know are not true?"
Joe Scarborough (*MSNBC – Morning Joe*) – November 16, 2015

Surely President Obama, acclaimed to be highly intelligent and a "quick study," must know and has heard the consensus of military leaders that his current level of military commitment to the War against ISIS will not end it before he leaves office – resulting in a stalemate at best.

Therefore, why now the nearly one-year delay in forming an alternative military strategy and a reluctance to make the necessary military commitment to win the War against ISIS by the Obama Administration? Lastly, in an October 2015 Associated Press-GFK Poll, even the American People disapproved of President Obama's timidity in meeting the ISIS threat thus far by a wide margin - 61% to 38%.

Indeed, *CNN* reported in September 2014 that President Obama admitted "*'we don't have a strategy'* to defeat ISIS. The President's remarks had followed days of speculation about whether the United States actually had a plan to go after ISIS in Syria."[69] Yet, even nine months later, in June 2015, President Obama still had no concrete strategy in place; "confessing *'we don't have a complete strategy'* yet for fighting the Islamic State:

> Nearly a year into the fight against ISIS, the U.S. still doesn't have a 'complete' strategy to end the terrorist group's bloody rampage across Iraq, President Obama admitted today (June 8, 2015)." Blaming the delay on the readiness (or lack thereof) of Iraq's army, President Obama added, *"'And so the details are not yet worked out'*...Once the Pentagon has provided him with a copy of the assessment, Obama said, he'll share it with the American People."[70] (Note: President Obama still has not yet shared the Pentagon report with the American People - nor has anyone in the media shown the curiosity to have even asked him why not).

Although, President Obama must accept the real possibility that he "is being played" by both Iran and the Baghdad government Iran backs to purposely slow-walk the preparedness of its Iraqi army. Frankly, so long as the Iraqi army never meets the Pentagon's minimum standard of readiness, President Obama and the U.S. military will remain at bay - at its current scant and precarious level of 5,000 U.S. troops in Iraq.

However, one must ask, why would Iran ever want to see the Iraqi army "ready" if it meant that President Obama and the Pentagon would finally give its military the green light to increase its U.S. troop presence in Iraq by tens of thousands of troops? Whereas, if the Iraqi army remains "unprepared" - thus keeping U.S. troops on the sidelines and out of Iraq - Iran alone will continue to dominate militarily and politically in Iraq. **Or is it perhaps just as plausible that President Obama really doesn't mind "being played" and is purposely using the Iraqi army "lack of readiness" issue as an alibi and pretext for delaying the introduction of significantly more U.S. troops to Iraq – thus avoiding any further escalation of the War against ISIS while he remains in office? Either way, however, Iran prevails.**

Ultimately, if President Obama still won't provide a more plausible explanation for his delay in responding strategically to the ISIS threat (now in year two), one hopes that it is something more than 1) his having to save face politically or 2) "to keep his *future political options* open" beyond 2016, as to specifically why he won't make the requisite military commitment to win the War against ISIS in Iraq – *now, before he leaves office.* **Otherwise, it is inevitable that, incrementally, tens of thousands more innocent civilians will die than need be while waiting out the last two years of the Obama Presidency for a new president to act.**

The Media's Mission

Always sympathetic to the Administration, the consensus of the liberal media is that, to his credit, President Obama simply does not believe war is a legitimate method of solving conflict. **But, reiterating again: What about Syria in 2013, when Mr. Obama – virtually by himself - was prepared to lead the charge to launch a punitive military strike against Syria for the killing of innocent men, women and children with chemical weapons. The only difference is** that, in 2015 in the War against ISIS – rather than chemical weapons – innocent men, women and children are being slaughtered instead with guns, beheaded with knives and machetes, drowned and burned alive, which is, in essence, no material distinction at all. So this "pacifist" defense of President Obama proffered by the mainstream media is without basis either.

We know that both the pliant mainstream media and the Democrats are predisposed and want to defend or "throw a lifeline" to Mr. Obama and his Administration wherever and whenever they can. But, in this instance, they too are, for the most part perplexed and on the sidelines. But not because they want to be. Indeed, David Axelrod, Bill Burton and *MSNBC* "stand at the ready." Further, it doesn't even matter how fantastic President Obama's explanation may be, so long as it 1) can't be disproven and 2) he sticks to it (e.g. he is still waiting on the readiness of the Iraq army).

Illustratively, regarding the IRS scandal, Obama insisted that he only learned of it through media reports. Although, before the scandal became public, accused IRS official Lois Lerner at the center of the scandal, had "planted" a question at a news briefing about the imminent first public release of an IRS Inspector General's report accusing the agency of targeting Conservative groups. In the real world, it defies credulity that Ms. Lerner, as also a loyal Democrat operative for many years, would not have at least advised her immediate superior and Obama Appointee, Attorney Williams Wilkens (i.e. Obama's "eyes and ears" at the IRS), who headed the IRS Headquarters' oversight Chief Counsel Office and that he, in turn would not have given the White House a "heads up."

Yet even today, the alibi stands that President Obama knew nothing until he heard about the IRS report in the media – no matter how fantastic and/or incompetent as that may sound in the short-term. And when all else fails, as President Obama's ever-sympathetic public advocate, probably still the mainstream media's most effective tool is to simply ignore a scandal and/or refuse to investigate it counting on that, with time, it will simply fade away.

The quintessential example of media bias is the feeding frenzy that erupted in 2015 wherein GOP Presidential Candidate Ben Carson was vilified by the mainstream media for 1) semantically mislabeling the financial "free ride" given to those attending West Point as "a scholarship" and 2) published recollections of Carson's youth that the media could not disprove. Therefore, the mainstream media concluded that Carson's recollections could not possibly be true which, ergo, seriously called into question Carson's credibility.

Whereas by stark contrast, during the 2012 Presidential Election, noted Obama author Mark Maraniss (even though an Obama acolyte) documented no less than 38 factual inaccuracies in the two books Barack Obama had written about himself. Yet, unlike Carson, the mainstream media never accused Barack Obama of being a "pathological liar" - hardly batting an eye and essentially ignoring the story during the Election.

However in the War against ISIS, President Obama needs to give the media something to work with - some plausible rationale that also would wash with the American People. If his refusal to ramp up the military effort to (in his words) "destroy and degrade" the ISIS menace is not because of political self-interest, President Obama has yet still to give the American People (or, for that matter, his political operatives) a more plausible rationale.

Finally, revealingly, how can President Obama justify such a limited U.S. military response to the ISIS threat in Iraq, especially in light of his September 2009 speech before the United Nations, when Mr. Obama himself insisted that the pursuit of peace by the United Nations *"must begin with an unshakable determination that the murder of innocent men, women and children will never be tolerated. On this, there can be no dispute."*

Syria and Chemical Weapons:

Why Obama "Allowed" Syria to Cross his "Red Line" Without Retribution:

Yet, by contrast to his reticence about fighting ISIS, concerning the deaths of hundreds of innocent civilians in Syria, Barack Obama displayed no such timidity regarding the August 2013 use of chemical weapons by Syria as a clear violation of international law demanding immediate retribution:

> *"I spent the last four and a half years doing everything I can to reduce our reliance on military power as a means of meeting our international obligations and protecting the American People. But what I also know is that there are times when we have to make a hard choice if we're going to stand up for the things we care about. I believe this is one of those times."*
> President Barack Obama – September 6, 2013

Throughout his Presidency, in fact, the only time that Barack Obama has strayed from strict adherence to the United Nations Multinational world dogma was in August 2013 when he boldly and emphatically "got out front," calling for a punitive military strike against Syria and its President, Basher al-Assad, for having used chemical weapons against his own people in violation of international human law. In fact, almost one year earlier to the day, President Obama had warned Syria that the use of chemical weapons in their civil war would cross Obama's self-declared "red line" calling for an immediate military response. As reported by *CNN:*

> Last week's (August 2013 chemical) attack obliterated the "red line" Obama set just over a year ago (in August 2012) against the use of Syria's chemical weapons stocks…Obama said he was determined to hold Syria accountable for using banned chemical weapons. *"It is not in the national security interests of the United States to ignore clear violations"* of what (President Obama) called an *"international norm,"* banning the use of chemical weapons.

> (President Obama) called the Syrian (chemical) attack a *"challenge to the world…My preference would have been that the international community already would have acted… A lot of people think something should be done, but nobody seems willing to do it"*… (Indeed), the White House had made clear that the United States will respond in some form to the use of chemical weapons…(In fact, Obama) and his top military and security aides are looking at a "limited, narrow action" to ensure that Syria and others know the United States and its allies won't tolerate similar future violations.[71]

President Obama wrongly assumed that, since Syria's use of chemical weapons was a clear violation of the "international norm," there would be enthusiastic and overwhelming support from the international community - i.e. the United Nations – to launch a "punitive" military strike against Syria in holding them responsible for their illegal actions in violation of international law. Further, President Obama unequivocally insisted that Bashar Assad must ultimately leave Syria (previously saying "his days are numbered.").

President Obama had even garnered the support of key Congressional leaders to back his proposed military action against Syria for having illegally used chemical weapons. Mr. Obama was adamant and poised to act. But, within two weeks, President Obama seemed to be suddenly backing off the military response that he had insisted was incumbent upon the international community to take against Syria's use of chemical weapons and for crossing his "red line." But why?

Yes, in the interim two weeks, Syrian President Assad had agreed to turn over his stockpile of chemical weapons in Syria. However, even if Assad allowed U.N. inspectors to oversee the removal of chemical weapons, there was no assurance that Assad or his military would not have secretly retained a cache of such prohibited weapons. In fact, in the two years-plus since Assad's agreement to turn over and destroy his entire chemical weapons stockpile, there have been innumerable reports of alleged chemical weapons attacks carried out by Syria, albeit on a lesser scale than the 1,400 killed in the initial August 2013 attack.

Although, Assad's standard response to all such instances of alleged use of chemical weapons by Syria has been to disavow responsibility by the Syrian government – rather, blaming the rebel insurgents for the chemical attacks instead. Yet, President Obama emphatically insisted that the U.S. intelligence evidence was indisputable as to Syria's responsibility for the initial August 2013 attack.

The Time Line (i.e. Who got to Obama Causing him to withdraw his "Red Line" Retaliation Threat against Syria?)

Friday, August 30, 2013
Morning - U.S. Secretary of State John Kerry (Statement)

1) "'This is common sense. These are facts.' John Kerry advanced what he called a 'clear and convincing' case that Syria

was responsible for a chemical attack that killed nearly 1,500 people [on August 21, 2013] in a statement on Friday that made clear the United States was on the verge of military attacks against the Assad regime." Additional Kerry quotes:

2) "'History will judge us all extraordinarily if we turn a blind eye to a dictator's wanton use of weapons of mass destruction.'"

3) "Kerry said that Iran could be 'emboldened' if the U.S. did not act."

4) Further, Kerry stated, "'It is about Hezbollah and North Korea and every other terrorist group that might ever again contemplate the use of weapons of mass destruction. Will they remember the Assad regime was stopped from those weapons' current or future use? Or will they remember that the world stood aside and created impunity?'"

5) "Kerry portrayed taking tough action as a matter of U.S. credibility, saying other countries that might use chemical weapons were watching. 'They want to see whether the United States and our friends mean what we say. It matters deeply to the credibility and the future of the United States of America and our allies.'" The Guardian news website "U.S. Set for Syria after Kerry says Evidence of Chemical Attacks 'clear'" - dated August 30, 2013

Friday, August 30, 2013
2:45 P.M. – President Barack Obama (Statement)

Later that day (at a White House Photo Op.), President Obama announces his intention to authorize a surgical military air strike against Syria in retribution for the use of chemical weapons killing over 1,400 of its own people on August 21, 2013. Only the time and locations of the attacks needed to be finalized. Quoting President Barack Obama:

1) "We cannot accept a world where women and children and innocent civilians are gassed on a terrible scale. This kind of attack threatens our National Security interests by violating well-established international norms against the use of chemical weapons."

2) ..."And it increases the risk that chemical weapons will be used in the future by terrorists who might use those weapons against us. The world has an obligation to maintain the norm against the use of chemical weapons."

3) "We are looking at the possibility of a limited, narrow act that would help make sure that not only Syria, but others around the world understand that the international community cares about maintaining this chemical weapons ban and norm."

Friday, August 30, 2013
6:00-6:45P.M. (Approximately Three Hours Later)

President Obama and his White House Chief of Staff Denis McDonough are observed taking an approximate 30-45-minute walk, commiserating in the White House Rose Garden.

Friday, August 30, 2013
(Shortly thereafter around the Dinner Hour)

President Obama telephones then-Defense Secretary Chuck Hagel.

Later relating the telephone conversation, Hagel indicated that he was stunned and astonished that President Obama told him to "stand down" – that the imminent military strike against Syria for using chemical weapons was "on hold" and as in later turned out, permanently.

Saturday, August 31, 2013
1:52 P.M. (A White House Press Release)

President Obama announces that he will not authorize a military strike against Syria without first obtaining the approval of Congress (which Obama knew would not be back in session for at least 7-10 days).

Given their respective speeches (on Friday August 30, 2013) calling for military retribution against Syria's use of chemical weapons banned by the International Community, could two men be any more in sync ("on the same page") on a particular issue, more adamant, with fortitude and resolve than President Barack Obama and Secretary of State John Kerry? Could any human being emphasize with greater certitude the absolute obligation and duty of the World Community to launch a punitive strike against Syria because, if it does not, according to President Obama "…it increases the risk that chemical weapons will be used in the future by terrorists who might use those weapons against us." Similarly, of the urgency and compulsion to act, Kerry added "'[H]istory will judge us all extraordinarily if we turn a blind eye to a dictator's wanton use of weapons of mass destruction.'"

That is until the approximate three-hour time period that day - between the time period 3-6 P.M. But what happened during this three-hour period that would cause President Obama

to inexplicably back off his "Red Line" military retaliation threat; for which he has been roundly criticized by not only his former Defense Secretary Leon Panetta but the prominent head of the bi-partisan Foreign Relations Council, Richard N. Haass – both of whom consider it the worst foreign policy blunder of Barack Obama's Presidency. There are only three possibilities: President Barack Obama was contacted by – or on behalf of - one of the following three people/governments and was advised to back off his "Red Line" military retaliation threat – which Obama did and why:

1) Vladimir Putin – Barack Obama was always sensitive and vulnerable to placating Putin; especially given A) Obama's hope for a second nuclear arms reduction agreement in his second term and B) the obvious need for the Russian President's acquiescence should Obama seek to become the next U.N. Secretary-General. It must be remembered that – after four and a half years into his Presidency by August 2013 – President Obama still had a decent working relationship with Putin, built primarily upon the one-side 2011 START Nuclear Arms Reduction Agreement (that heavily favored Russia according to *The Heritage Foundation*). **That is until the relationship blew up for good six months later, in March 2014, with the Russian invasion and annexation of Crimea.** However, regarding Obama's "Red Line" threat against Syria, it would seem that if Putin vehemently objected to Obama's intention to launch a one-time military strike – causing Putin to possibly threaten military intervention on Syria's behalf – that, diplomatically, Putin would not have waited until the "Eleventh Hour" to privately make known his objections.

2) Iran – Journalist Jay Solomon (Wall Street Journal) contends that, based on his anonymous sources, it was the Iranians that let it be known that they would end negotiations for a Nuclear Deal if President Obama followed through with his anticipated military air attack on Iran's ally Syria. Ultimately, it was determined that President Obama, from the outset, had another personal legacy ambition and insistence to see to it that a Nuclear Deal was eventually struck with Iran (no matter how hollow or one-sided). Consequently, it is plausible that Obama could have been so abruptly cowered into permanently calling off his "Red Line" attack at the last minute by such a threat from Iran – despite the ensuing criticism that Obama would subsequently endure both domestically and worldwide for doing so. However, remember: That very same day, Secretary Kerry had declared and cautioned that, alternatively, "Iran could be 'emboldened' if the U.S. did not act." Finally, for what it's worth, not surprisingly, the White House vehemently denied that Iran played any role in President Obama's subsequent decision to permanently call off his "Red Line" punitive military strike against Syria.

3) Ban Ki-moon – United Nations Secretary-General Ban Ki-moon did not publically come out against President Obama's intention to launch a punitive military strike against Syria (advising that it would be a violation of International Law) until September 4, 2013; four days after President Obama's August 30, 2013 pronouncement. However, given their close relationship and, more importantly, reports that the military strike could occur as soon as the next day (Saturday), one would have certainly expected that the U.N. Secretary-General, without delay, would have made his objections known to Obama before Saturday and prior to his public

statement four days later. Secondly, by providing Obama a "heads-up," it allowed President Obama, in the interim, to fashion the cover story that he suddenly (for once) actually cared about having Congressional approval for his proposed Executive military action - but only as merely a pretense to buy time (which Obama, in fact, did the very next day, Saturday, August 31, 2013).

No matter which of the above scenarios actually occurred, it is unsettling to say the least, that a President of the United States would either 1) cower in the face of a direct threat from Vladimir Putin or Iran or 2) allow personal legacy ambitions to take precedence (i.e. securing a future Iranian Nuclear Deal or ingratiating himself with the U.N. Secretary-General in hopes of one day garnering his support to become U.N. Secretary-General) at the expense of the prestige of the United States that even John Kerry said - that same day - would be lost with both allies and adversaries worldwide if "the world stood aside" and did nothing.

Specifically regarding United Nations Secretary-General Ban Ki-moon's warning against a "punitive" military strike on Syria for its alleged use of chemical weapons against its own people, in no uncertain terms, Ban Ki-moon cautioned that such a unilateral, punitive military strike by one nation or a group of nations against another would also be a violation of international law – without, at least, the prior approval of the United Nations Security Council:

> *"As I have repeatedly said, the [U.N.] Security Council has primary responsibility for international peace and security. The use of force is only exercised in self-defense, in accordance with Article 51 of the U.N. Charter or when the Security Council approves such action."* Moreover, he

warned that a military strike against Syria could unleash (even) more turmoil and bloodshed in a crisis that had already killed more than 100,000 people.[72]

Rather, to peaceably resolve the issue, Ban Ki-moon ultimately asked the U.N. Security Council to demand that the Syrian government turn over its entire stock of chemical weapons, adding:

If U.N. inspectors confirm the use of chemical weapons in Syria, it would be an *"abominable crime"* worthy of international response – but Ban Ki-moon had previously also warned against *"further militarization of the conflict"* in Syria."[73]

Suddenly turning on a dime, within a week of the U.N. Secretary-General's admonishment, *CNN* reported that "facing weak support for U.S. military action, President Obama (on September 10, 2013) said that a plan to have Syria hand its chemical arsenal over to international control could avert American strikes, 'If it's real.' "[74] But was it Assad's promise to turn over his stockpile of chemical weapons that really caused Barack Obama to abruptly abandon his vow to launch punitive air strikes against Syria?

Or is it not more likely Barack Obama, once again, dutifully took his cue from U.N. Secretary-General Ban Ki-moon a week earlier and backed off his previously unwavering declaration to punish Syria with punitive military strikes - using the Russian-backed plan as (in his mind) a convenient pretext. However, no matter 1) what the personal ridicule and embarrassment he would face (and is still enduring) for not following through and enforcing his "red line" edict and 2) the accompanying loss in credibility and prestige that the United States would suffer as a result, did Barack Obama reason that it was still more in his best legacy interest – and a potential shot at becoming a U.N. Secretary-General in the future - to quickly "get on board" with the current thinking of the U.N. Secretary-General's unequivocal U.N. policy warning advising against any punitive military strike by the United States against Syria?

In less than two weeks, President Obama had went from vehemently insisting that *"It is not in the national security interests of the United States to ignore"* the Syrian chemical attack that killed more than 1,400 people to compliantly kowtowing to U.N. Secretary-General Ban Ki-moon's admonition to back off his "Red Line" declaration against Syria.

Where Obama Went Wrong:

During the first seven years of his Presidency, Barack Obama has suffered no greater foreign policy humiliation than for his vow to punish Syria for crossing his "red line" by using chemical weapons - in violation of international law – but, ultimately, backing off and never following through. Neither Conservatives nor Liberals could understand or explain Mr. Obama's motivation in abruptly backing off his determination to see to it that Syria, and Bashar Al-Assad in particular, were militarily punished for having used chemical weapons.

Both Republicans and a number of Democrats heaped criticism on Mr. Obama, but probably none more devastating and representative than the blistering criticism from his own former Defense Secretary (2011-2013) and prominent Democrat Leon Panetta. As previously referenced, "[f]ormer Defense Secretary Leon Panetta said that President Obama damaged United States security by drawing a "red line" against Syria's use of chemical weapons and then failing to back it up with military force when Syria crossed it:

> *"I think the credibility of the United States is on the line. It is important for us to stand by the world and going in and doing what a Commander-in-Chief should do. [But] Mr. Obama sent a mixed message, not only to Assad, not only to the Syrians, but to the world..."*

"Mr. Obama instead opted for a Russian-backed disarmament plan after Mr. Assad, tightening his grip on power in the face of a popular uprising and civil war, used chemical weapons to kill as many as 1,400 people."[75]

Similarly and almost verbatim, (as previously noted) the highly respected President of the non-partisan Council on Foreign Relations, Richard Haass, speaking critically of President Obama's failure to enforce his "red line" ultimatum to the Syrian government for using chemical weapons stated:

> *"[President Obama's] credibility has taken a major hit. Probably the most consequential thing that he didn't do in his Presidency was to follow up on his pledge to attack the [Assad] regime after they used chemical weapons. And that had consequences not just in Syria, not just the Middle East, but throughout the world.*[76]

President Obama made a series of blunders and miscalculations in his assumption that world opinion, led by the United Nations, would enthusiastically follow his lead and support a punitive military strike against Syria for crossing his "red line" by using chemical weapons:

1. President Obama must have assumed that the United Nations and U.N. Secretary-General Ban Ki-moon in particular, would readily accept the finding of U.S. intelligence, assessing with 90% certainty that Syria, indeed, was solely responsible for the chemical attack and not the insurgents as Assad claimed. Apparently, President Obama never even considered the possibility that the United Nations would balk; even after its long-standing heightened skepticism of U.S. intelligence reliability engendered by the 2003 so-called "failure of intelligence" that Iraq possessed WMD as justification for the Iraq War. Further, given that U.N. inspectors in Syria had no mandate to determine clear responsibility for the chemical attack, once Assad counter-claimed that the insurgents were to blame, U.N. Secretary-General Ban Ki-moon refused to support President Obama's proposal for a punitive military strike.

2. Nor did President Obama consider or know of the heightened concern of U.N. Secretary-General Ban Ki-moon that such a military strike might only further escalate the Syrian civil war and death toll.

3. Ultimately, President Obama must have been shocked that only three nations (Jordan, Turkey and Israel) publically declared support for his proposal to launch a punitive strike against Syria; whereas the Arab League, NATO and the European Union (including even Great Britain) refused to support him.

4. Moreover, President Obama must have known ahead of his announcement that, at a minimum, Russia and probably China – both as allies of Syria – would veto any

attempt to pass a United Nations Security Council resolution sanctioning a punitive military strike against the Syrian government even if it was proven, to the satisfaction of the U.N., that Assad was responsible.

Obama Must Concede to Russia, China and Article 51

Regarding his refusal over the years to support the rebel and insurgent forces with direct U.S. military intervention against the government of Syria, President Obama stood alone in opposition to leaders in his own Administration – not the least of which were Secretary of State Hillary Clinton and Secretary of Defense Leon Panetta. However, because of his lockstep adherence to United Nations dogma in conducting U.S. foreign policy, President Obama knew and accepted that he was bound and precluded from acting against Assad precisely by Article 51 of the United Nations Charter, that, reiterating, states in the absence of a resolution supported by the U.N. Security Council (for which both Russia and China would have most assuredly exercised their veto power), a nation or nations can only launch military strikes against another in "self-defense." Consequently, President Obama had no choice but to accept the box that Article 51 put him in and stand down on his "red line" declaration.

But, granting President Obama the benefit of doubt, in his rush to be out front in advocating a punitive military strike against Syria for using chemical weapons, he may have finally been prone to act and caved to (and now most assuredly regrets) the repeated ardent support by his "inside-the-administration" advisors for some sort of military response on behalf of Syrian rebels and insurgents. Moreover, President Obama, at the time, most likely (and erroneously) perceived that this obvious violation of international law by Syria (which even Russia and China would not be able to defend) may have been his one and only opportunity that he would, therefore ever have to placate and simultaneously quell his critics – on both the left and right in his Administration and Congress - as to his failure before then (and since) to, in some demonstrative manner, show military support for the opposition in Syria.

Intriguingly, in assessing Barack Obama as a leader of the free world, Hillary Clinton squarely blamed the President for the rise of ISIS in Syria and Iraq - making the following observation about Obama's foreign policy leadership style:

> (Clinton) suggested that she finds (President Obama's) approach overly cautious, and she made the case that America needs a leader who believes that the country, despite its various missteps, is an indispensable force for good...[S]he repeatedly suggested that the United States appears to be withdrawing from the world stage.[77]

Indeed, more than one year after Mr. Obama's 'red line' Syrian foreign policy fiasco, in November 2014 regarding ISIS in Iraq, Michael T. Klare of the decidedly left-leaning *The Nation* magazine observed that President Obama was just as, if not more, reticent to become more than mildly involved in military intervention – even where the United Nations would not object (i.e. to the fight against ISIS). "Although Obama has been noticeably reluctant to become-involved in Iraq, Syria and Ukraine, he is coming under pressure from Democrats and Republicans to employ tougher measures in all three."[78]

Throughout the Obama Presidency, the renown *Washington Post* journalist and expert on U.S. foreign policy, David Ignatius has been supportive of the President. However, apparently he too was perplexed and at a lost to explain President Obama's demonstrated tentative and less than robust response in the war against ISIS and in Syria (*MSNBC Morning Joe* - November 25, 2015).

Specifically concerning Syria, neither David Ignatius nor anyone else in the media – Liberal or Conservative - has ever suggested that, in actuality, it is Barack Obama's self-imposed strict adherence to Article 51 and the inevitable Security Council opposition of Russia and China that precludes him from directly intervening militarily on behalf of the Syrian rebels and insurgents against the Syrian government. And although the mainstream media fails to recognize it, Vladimir Putin knows it and counts on it. Reiterating: To suggest otherwise would be a violation of international law and U.N. Secretary-General Ban Ki moon has already slapped President Obama down once for even considering it. Notwithstanding Syrian leader Assad's culpability in the brutal killing of over 250,000 of his own people.

Moreover, given that there is nothing in it for either Putin or Assad, the chances for an Obama Administration hoped-for meaningful, long-term political settlement between the Syrian government and the rebel opposition in the near future are remote at best. Bluntly, any political settlement would be antithetical to Putin's goal of establishing a permanent foothold and sphere of influence in the Middle East – something Russia has not had in over 40 years. Only when ISIS is defeated in both Iraq and Syria will the United States have any leverage in Syria - coupled with a new President who does not choose to allow himself to be bound by the restrictions of Article 51 of the United Nations Charter. Although, again, if Barack Obama's motivation or rationale is otherwise, he has yet to reveal it.

Lastly, at a rally in January 2016, Donald Trump was ridiculed by

Hillary Clinton, who insinuated that he had fabricated a claim that President Obama and she, as then-Secretary of State, were responsible for the rise of ISIS. The irony - which the media and even Trump failed to pick up on - is that it was not Trump; but Hillary Clinton, over a year earlier, who was actually the first person to, in effect, suggest that Barack Obama was responsible for the rise of ISIS (see Footnote 77: August 10, 2014 - *The Atlantic*). Remember: At the time, it was Barack Obama who stood alone – in opposition to the advice of the heads of his National Security team - arguing against arming the Syrian rebels. Indeed, the very header that appears at the top of each page throughout the August 10, 2014 *The Atlantic* report by Jeffrey Goldberg is entitled "Hillary Clinton: 'Failure' to help Syrian rebels led to the rise of ISIS."

But Syria Still Possesses Chemical Weapons Even Today

On September 29, 2015, White House spokesman Josh Ernest contended that President Obama was actually right in backing off his 2013 "red line" threat, in that it served as the catalyst that led to the Russian-backed deal that caused Assad to give up his entire "declared" (Ernest parsed his words carefully) stockpile of chemical weapons - whereas merely a one-time military strike would not have.[79]

However, in fact, there appears to be recent evidence that Syria still possesses chemical weapon stockpiles in clear violation of its claims to have complied with the United Nations to have relinquished all of its chemical weapons, according to a *Reuters* news report (republished by *Townhall.com "By the Way, Syria Habitually Violating Obama's 'Red Line' Deal"* –May 13, 2015). In December 2014-January 2015, the Organization for Prohibition of Chemical Weapons (OPCW) inspectors found samples of both sarin and VX chemical gas still present in Syria:

" 'This is a pretty good indication they have been lying about what they did with the sarin' one diplomatic source said. 'They have so far been unable to give a satisfactory explanation about this finding.' "

Although, keeping a decidedly low-profile on this discovery, Secretary of State John Kerry subsequently brokered a deal wherein Syria, without any penalty whatsoever, agreed to identify and turn over all chemical gases and weapons pertaining to this singular instance to resolve the issue without any further international 'red line' public controversy (Apparently White House spokesman Ernest was unaware of this *Reuters News* account that occurred just four months earlier).

(Moreover according to the *Reuters*), Syria has four chemical weapons factories that they never disclosed to the United Nations, a Western diplomat told *CNN*. The diplomat, Sigrid Kaag, the U.N. Special Envoy overseeing the destruction of Syria's chemical stockpiles, briefed the U.N. Security Council. The new *Reuters* report cited above demonstrates that the (Syrian) regime never had any intention of abiding by their obligations under the agreement, and they've evidently determined they have little to fear in the way of U.S. reprisals.

But now what will President Obama do? Most probably, nothing - unless Ban Ki-Moon changes his mind first (i.e. perhaps if, in the future, the U.N. Secretary-General becomes convinced that Syria is, indeed, responsible for the continued widespread use of chemical weapons). Remember that it took only seven days for President Obama to get the signal the last time (i.e. cancelling his proposed punitive Syrian military strike). He will not make his one and only mistake again in misreading the intentions of the United

Nations and U.N. Secretary Ban Ki-moon in particular, during the remainder of his Presidency.

Bluntly, President Obama is effectively handcuffed by U.N. Secretary General Ban Ki moon and precluded from intervening in any meaningful way that could even be remotely construed as opposing the sitting Syrian government of Bashar Assad. As a consequence of A) being admonished once already by the U.N. Secretary-General in September 2013 (i.e. Obama backing off his Red Line warning) and B) at the risk of tarnishing his pristine image in Ban Ki moon's eyes as a dutiful peacemaker, President Obama apparently accepts the constraints of Article 51 that bind and prevent him from overtly supporting the Syrian opposition. Thus, President Obama has no leverage at all in negotiations with Putin to effect a peaceful settlement to remove Assad.

Finally, according to Syrian Rebel General Abdul Hadi Isari who has been responsible for supplying the Syrian insurgents with weapons to fight Assad, in all there have been no less than 78 smaller-scale chemical weapons attacks on the Syrian people carried out by the Syrian Government since the initial major attack in August 2013. However, now General Isari says that the Assad military is technically skirting international law by switching to Chlorine gas dropped from helicopters. Although, according to President Obama, Chlorine gas, albeit deadly, is not technically a chemical weapon:

> *"It's true that we've seen reports of the use of chlorine in bombs that had the effect of chemical weapons. Chlorine itself historically has not been listed as a chemical weapon. But when it is used in this fashion can be considered a prohibited use of that chemical."*
> President Barack Obama – May 14, 2015

However, it still has never been explained to the Syrian people in opposition to Assad's government why President Obama has repeatedly over the years allowed Assad to cross his "red line" and then failed to enforce it by coming to the aid of the insurgents – instead apparently acquiescing to the brokered deal with Russia in which Assad ostensibly claims to have turned over his entire chemical weapons arsenal to be destroyed by the international community.[80] Ultimately, it is incumbent upon President Obama to tell the American People and the Syrian people in opposition why he and his Administration are apparently okay with the 79 chemical attacks that have occurred to date and now the continued unfettered use of Chlorine gas by the Assad government.

An Even Greater U.S. Foreign Policy Disaster than Obama Failing to Enforce his "Red Line"?

> "Why are we abandoning helping [Syrian] refugees at home and descending into this 'vetting/no vetting' quagmire?"
> Waled Pharis, a Leading Expert on Middle Eastern Affairs (and a Donald Trump Foreign Policy Advisor) – *Fox News "Your World with Neil Cavuto"* – August 18, 2016

Prominent Middle Eastern Expert Waled Pharis noted that, in Syria, while there are now (in 2016) more than 400,000 dead in the Syrian civil war, there are more than four million refugees who have already left Syria seeking asylum throughout Europe and America, while another seven million Syrians remain homeless and displaced within the borders of their own country. Pharis believes President Obama's failure to intervene in Syria (not offensively against the Assad regime but in a defensive-humanitarian effort) to provide secure Safe Zones and refugee camps for all Syrian refugees, could one day prove to be a catastrophic worldwide security threat.

As a solution, Pharis noted that currently the Hasaka area of Syria controlled by the Kurds could accommodate millions of Syrian refugees precluding the necessity for them to seek refuge abroad. Moreover, Pharis stated that Hasaka is 10,000 square kilometers in area and equivalent in size to the country of Lebanon.

Since at least 2013, President Obama has interpreted the constraints of U.N. Article 51 as precluding him (without U.N. Security Council approval) from interceding offensively against the Assad regime in power in Syria. Even though in 2011, President Obama's position singularly put him at odds with virtually every head of his U.S. National Security team – including his former Secretaries of Defense and State (Panetta and Clinton), former CIA Director Petraeus and the former Joint Chief of Staff Martin Dempsey. Secondly, President Obama fears that even a humanitarian effort to establish Safe Zones could end up drawing the United States directly into the Syria conflict.

However, a humanitarian effort to establish and act militarily to strictly protect and defend Safe Zones within Syria from attack would not be a violation of Article 51. And President Obama could have begun doing this four years ago but chose not to. Had he, it would have significantly stemmed the flood of "The Great Migration" of the four million-plus refugees from Syria across Europe and America – and at a much lower cost by keeping them in their own homeland than, for example, the projected $130,000 per refugee cost for each of the 10,000 Syrian refugees transported and resettled in the U.S. just in 2016 (according to Robert Rector of the *Heritage Foundation*).

Although, of even greater concern than financial is the National Security risk to not only the United States but throughout Europe - given the practical inability to properly vet these people. Democrats and the Obama Administration will counter, arguing that 1) the preliminary vetting process of refugees performed by the United Nations and 2) the well-established two-year U.S. immigration vetting process are both sufficient. However, it is said by critics that the vetting process performed by the United Nations is superficial at best. And the vastly more stringent two-year U.S. immigration vetting process wasn't even applied (when "push came to shove") to the first 10,000 Syrian refugees whom President Obama wanted settled in this country over an even shorter six-month period, by the end of September 2016.

Ultimately, the global security of the Western World will be even more at risk for years and perhaps decades to come because President Obama lacked the foresight to recognize the potential magnitude of this specific security risk to the world – even if only 1% of all Syrian refugees become ISIS-infiltrated jihadists. However, note that just 1% of 4 million Syrian refugees is still 40,000 committed jihadi terrorists. Of course, we may not know for a period of 10-20 years (long after President Obama has left the White House) the degree of the terrorist threat throughout the world that has been wrought by President Obama who remains hamstrung by his conscious adherence to Article 51 and his self-proclaimed doctrine of "Leading from Behind."

In the meantime, President Obama's "hands off" approach as it pertains to Syria has not escaped Syrian President Assad's gaze. Indeed, before President Obama leaves office in January 2017, Assad is feverishly stepping up the attack upon all rebel-held areas of Syria – and Aleppo in particular – in hopes of consolidating a permanent stranglehold against the Opposition.

_____

CHAPTER 7

[65] *Washington Post* "Obama at Arlington on Memorial Day Pays Tribute for a 'Debt that can Never be Fully Repaid'" by Steven Mufson – May 25, 2015.

[66] *The Daily Beast* "Exclusive: 50 Spies Say ISIS Intelligence Was Cooked" by Shane Harris and Nancy A. Youssef – September 9, 2015.

[67] *Fox News-The Kelly File* – Interview: U.S. Army Lieutenant Colonel (Retired) Anthony Shaffer – September 10, 2015.

[68] *National Journal* "What Would Obama of 2007 Say About his War Powers Request?" by George E. Condon Jr. – February 11, 2015.

[69] *CNN* "Obama on ISIS in Syria 'We Don't Have a Strategy'" by Chelsea J. Carter, Catherine E. Shoichet and Hamdi Alkhshali – September 4, 2014.

[70] *The Daily Mail* "Obama: 'We Don't Yet Have a Strategy' to Stop ISIS in Iraq" by Francesca Chambers – June 8, 2015.

[71] *CNN* – " 'War-Weary' Obama Says Syria Chemical Attack Requires Response" by Frederick Pleitgen and Tom Cohen – August 30, 2013.

[72] *The WorldPost* "U.S. Strike in Syria Could Unleash More Turmoil, UN Chief Ban Ki-moon Says" by Peter James Spielmann – September 3, 2013.

[73] *CNN* "Syria Chemical Arms Plan Promising 'If it's real' Obama Says" by Matt Smith and Catherine E. Shoichet – September 10, 2013.

[74] *CNN* – Ibid – September 10, 2013.

[75] *The Washington Times* "The Knives are Out: Panetta Eviscerates Obama's 'Red Line' Blunder on Syria" by S.A. Miller – October 7, 2014.

[76] *MSNBC* – *Morning Joe* – September 29, 2015.

[77] *The Atlantic* "Hillary Clinton: 'Failure' to Help Syrian Rebels Led to the Rise of ISIS" by Jeffrey Goldberg – August 10, 2014.

[78] *The Nation* "The Real Reason Defense Secretary Chuck Hagel Got Booted" by Michael T. Klare – November 26, 2014.

[79] *MSNBC* "*Morning Joe*" – September 29, 2015.

[80] *Fox News Reporting* "Crossing Jordan – Escape from Terror" by Bret Baier – June 26, 2015.

Barack Obama's Performance as the World Peacemaker-in-Waiting - Re: Russia, China and Iran

It is widely held that the United States and Russia control more than 90% of all nuclear weapons worldwide.

Throughout his Presidency, there has been a conscious effort made by Barack Obama's political handlers in the Administration to promote the President's image on the world stage – above all – as that of a non-confrontational world peacemaker. In April 2009, just three months after taking office, Mr. Obama stated that his primary nuclear policy objective as President was to strive for and promote nuclear non-proliferation worldwide and a world, ultimately, "without nuclear weapons" (Note the similarity of phases and words used by President Obama to those of Secretaries-General Ban Ki-moon and Kofi Annan to follow, which have been underlined herein):

> *"As the only nuclear power to have used a weapon – the United States has a moral responsibility to act...So, today, I state clearly and with conviction America's commitment to seek the peace and security of <u>a world without nuclear weapons</u>. I'm not naïve. This goal will not be reached*

quickly – perhaps not in my lifetime. It will take patience and persistence…The United States will take concrete steps toward <u>a world without nuclear weapons</u>. "
Barack Obama, President of the United States – Prague, Czechoslovakia – April 5, 2009

Certainly a laudable theoretical notion, if not practicable, because where vacuums of power exist in the world, evil and bad actors will appear to fill them. **Even more revealing, however, Mr. Obama's "world without nuclear weapons" phraseology parallels the exact sentiments and coded language of both former U.N. Secretary-General Kofi Annan and the current Secretary-General Ban Ki-moon:**

Kofi Annan

In 2005, then-Secretary-General Kofi Annan said every nation must work toward *"a world of reduced nuclear threat and, ultimately, <u>a world free of nuclear weapons</u>"*…He also called on <u>the U.S. and Russia to cut back even more sharply on their (nuclear) arsenals.</u>[81]

Ban Ki-moon

"Together we have a dream about <u>a nuclear-free world</u>. Now we must act to achieve it…The need for action is clear. Thousands of nuclear weapons remain on hair-trigger alert. "
Ban Ki-moon, who also said he had long advocated for a stronger role for the U.N. Security Council in Nuclear Non-Proliferation Disarmament – "The United Nations Summit on Efforts to End Nuclear Weapons Proliferation" – September 24, 2009

"Together, we are on a journey from Ground Zero to Global

> *Zero – <u>a world free of weapons of mass destruction</u>. That is the only sane path to a safer world."*
> Ban Ki-moon, Hiroshima Park – August 6, 2010

> *"Let us demand an end to all nuclear tests, get on with the unfinished business of achieving <u>a world free of nuclear weapons</u> and usher in a safer and more prosperous future."*
> Ban Ki-moon – August 24, 2014

Just as striking is the linkage – in commitment, actions and verbiage - between Barack Obama and 1) Ban Ki-moon's October 2008 Five Point Nuclear Disarmament Plan entitled "United Nations and Security in <u>a Nuclear-Weapons-Free-World</u>" and 2) Ban Ki-moon's support for and urging that the United States ratify the Comprehensive Nuclear-Test-Ban Treaty (CTBT), which according to the U.N. Secretary-General is integral to implementing his Five Point Nuclear Disarmament Plan:

The Five-Point Nuclear Disarmament Plan

Ban Ki-moon (October 24, 2008)

> *1. The Nuclear Non-Proliferation Treaty remains a cornerstone of global disarmament and non-proliferation regime. I urge all NPT parties, in particular the nuclear-weapons-states, to fulfill their obligation under the Treaty to undertake negotiations on effective measures leading to nuclear disarmament...The world would also welcome <u>a resumption of bilateral negotiations between the United States and [the] Russian Federation</u> aimed at <u>deep and verifiable reductions of their respective [nuclear] arsenals</u>.*

2. *[The CTBT] relates to the "rule of law." <u>Unilateral moratoria</u> on nuclear tests and the production <u>of fissile materials</u> can only go so far. We need new efforts to bring the CTBT into force [i.e. ratification by all nations].*

Ban Ki-moon (September 24, 2009)

"[President Obama] pledged that the United States would host a Summit in 2010 and pursue <u>deep cuts in its nuclear arsenal</u>, as well as <u>agreements with the Russian Federation towards the elimination of nuclear weapons.</u>"

Compared to Barack Obama (April 2009)

1. *"To put an end to Cold War thinking, <u>we will reduce the role of nuclear weapons</u> in our national security strategy and urge others to do the same. We will begin the work of <u>reducing our arsenal</u>. To reduce our warheads and stockpiles, <u>we will negotiate a new strategic arms treaty [i.e. the eventual 2011 New START Treaty] with Russia this year.</u>"*

2. *[Regarding the CTBT], to achieve a ban on nuclear testing, <u>my Administration will immediately and aggressively pursue U.S. ratification of the Comprehensive Test Ban Treaty</u>. After more than five decades of talks, it is time for the testing of nuclear weapons to finally be banned."* (However, by January 18, 2013, the U.S. had yet to ratify the CTBT causing Ban Ki-moon to announce that he would be traveling to the United States to meet with President Obama to urge immediate ratification – but, it has yet to occur)

3. *"And to cut off the building blocks needed for a bomb,*

the United States will seek a new treaty that <u>verifiably ends the production of fissile materials</u> intended for use in state nuclear weapons."

Barack Obama (White House Statement – March 5, 2015)

1. *"As I stated in Prague in 2009, reinforced in Berlin in 2013, and again reaffirmed last month in my National Security Strategy, the United States seeks the peace and security of <u>a world without nuclear weapons</u>. We encourage all states to strengthen the NPT as a basis for cooperation to achieve that shared goal...Our commitment to Non-Proliferation is at the center of our efforts.*

2. *[Regarding his own perceived achievements:] "During my Administration, the United States has <u>reduced the role nuclear weapons</u> play in our security <u>and reduced the size of our arsenal</u>...Under New START and in conformity with our NPT obligations, we are <u>reducing our strategic nuclear weapon stockpile</u> to the lowest level in more than a half a century, and <u>we are prepared to negotiate further reductions,</u> while protecting our security and that of our friends and allies around the world."*

1. Russia: The New START Treaty as Leverage for Putin

Indeed two years before Vladimir Putin's takeover of Crimea, in early 2012 the Obama Administration announced that it was considering yet another stage of nuclear warhead cuts with Russia sometime after the 2012 Presidential Election year, according to Ellen Tascher, a senior State Department arms-control officer. Moreover:

> The Associated Press reported that the (Obama) Administration is weighing options for potential deep cuts in the number of deployed long-range nuclear weapons, including the possibility of dipping to as low as 300 to 400 long-range nuclear warheads.[82]

However now, with "near certainty," there will be no further reductions in the United States nuclear arsenal during the remainder of Barack Obama's Presidency – even if he desperately wants one to further his Presidential legacy – because of Russian President Putin's 2014 annexation of Crimea and his de facto occupation of eastern Ukraine. Even if President Obama thought he could somehow still pull it off after the 2014 Mid-Term Elections, the chances of another treaty being approved now by the Republican-controlled U.S. Senate are virtually non-existent.

Ironically, thwarting President Obama's zeal to further reduce our nuclear arsenal is probably the only "good" to have come out of the deplorable Russian invasion of Ukraine. And that is not insignificant, as it will serve to maintain and insure what current U.S. edge remains in the global nuclear military Balance of Power between the two countries.

Crystalizing the crux of the dispute about U.S. and Russian nuclear stockpiles, throughout his presidency, George W. Bush was adamant about not reducing U.S. nuclear warhead strength below 2,200, as a necessary minimum nuclear deterrent to Russia. Whereas, according to the nuclear warhead reduction entered into in the 2011 New START treaty, President Obama agreed to reduce nuclear warheads from 2,200 down to 1,550. Moreover, Mr. Obama's goal before his presidency ends was to further reduce all nuclear warheads to at least below 1,000 – and even as low as 300-400 long-range nuclear warheads, according to some in his Administration. Then came the Crimea takeover and the de facto occupation of eastern Ukraine by Vladimir Putin that continues today.

Concerns about Further Cuts in the U.S. Nuclear Arsenal

Prior to the 2015 Iran Nuclear Deal, President Obama's signature foreign policy "achievement" was, according to his Administration, the 2011 New START nuclear weapons "reduction" agreement with Russia. However, reiterating according to *The Heritage Foundation*, in fact, the New START agreement will in theory A) allow Russia to potentially "increase," rather than decrease, its nuclear warheads from 1,550 back to 2,200, as well as B) allow Russia, for the first time, to launch ICBMs from mobile aircraft rather than from previously identified (i.e. known) land-based stationary sites only.[83]

And if *The Heritage Foundation* was already against the 2011 New START agreement that reduced the U.S. nuclear arsenal from 2,200 to 1,550, needless to say, it ardently rejects any further such reductions below the 1,550 level – much less the Obama Administration's consideration of a proposal to permanently reduce U.S. long-range nuclear warheads to as low as 300-400.

Moreover, what about consideration for the level of strength of the U.S. nuclear weapon deterrent versus the level and growth of China's nuclear arsenal today? The non-partisan Council on Foreign Relations - which has generally been supportive of President Obama's foreign policy throughout his presidency - made the following observation (although not endorsing it) of those who criticize the consideration of any further cuts to the U.S. nuclear warhead arsenal:

The United States also needs to be mindful of threats from great power countries like Russia and China. Russia, despite acceding to the New START Treaty in 2011, still has a larger arsenal than the United States, and even threatened to target U.S. plans for a strengthened missile defense system in Europe. In addition, reports have emerged that China's nuclear arsenal is substantially larger than originally projected and growing.[84]

Obama's "Achilles Heel" in Dealing with Putin:[85]

"Although, the real concern now is to what extent President Obama might be vulnerable and, thus, could be intimidated or constrained in responding to further Russian military aggression - given Putin's threat (during the 2014 Russian incursion into Ukraine) to negate or suspend the ratified (New START) nuclear arms treaty negotiated between the two men and signed in 2011. The problem here is that Putin knows President Obama views the 2011 New START Treaty as his signature foreign policy objective and achievement during his first term and, therefore just how much it means to Mr. Obama that the treaty remain intact.

Natural Gas as a Weapon

According to the Federal Government's non-partisan Congressional Research Service (August 20, 2013), "successive Administrations and Congresses have viewed European energy security as a U.S. National Security Interest…The Obama Administration has called for (European natural gas) diversification, but has refrained from openly expressing concerns about Russia's (dominate natural gas) regional policy, perhaps in order to avoid jeopardizing relations with Moscow."

However, just what has President Obama's Nuclear Weapons Reduction policy really accomplished? The Russian invasion of the Crimean province of Ukraine illustratively reveals just how much the United States' European allies are, in effect, handcuffed and stymied from responding in any meaningful way - due in no small part to European dependence on Russian natural gas. Moreover, since 2009, President Obama's largely futile attempts at appeasing Vladimir Putin have, thus essentially accomplished nothing towards the goal of advancing the development of a European natural gas alternative (i.e. five years wasted).

But, why not export U.S. domestic natural gas to the Europeans? Well, Obama's EPA, throughout the first five years of his presidency, "slow-walked" applications for over 20 new natural gas pipelines - while approving only two. Bluntly, whether it's the development of an alternative natural gas pipeline in Europe or expanding U.S. natural gas production to supplant Russian dependency, President Obama will not really even consider either possibility because a natural gas solution that relies primarily on a carbon-based resource and the fracking extraction method is still an anathema to 1) the Climate Change Environmental Movement - to which the President and the Democrat Party are so beholden and 2) United Nations Climate Change policy. President Obama isn't going to do it. Politically, he can't do it. NATO and the National Security of Europe and the American People be damned.

Moreover, note that the Environmental Protection Agency recently affirmed that there would be a two-year lead-time necessary to even adequately begin supplying Europe with its natural gas needs. Thus, had President Obama made the export sale of U.S. domestically-produced natural gas legal when he came into office, Europe's current dependence on Russia could have at least begun to be eliminated

four years ago. **In the 21st century, eliminating European dependence on Russian natural gas is just as important as the military
might of NATO was in the 20th century - in securing European
and U.S. National Security."**

2. China: What about Currency Manipulation and Cyber Espionage?

Donald Trump: Right on China, but Absolutely the Wrong Messenger[86]

"Donald Trump is absolutely correct that the U.S. trade policy towards China over the last 20 years has been timid at best - during
both Democrat and Republican Administrations. And the blatant
manipulation of its own currency by the government of China, indeed, has had the practical effect of erecting protective tariff trade
barriers making it virtually impossible for foreign goods exported to
China from the United States to fairly compete.

Trump's bluster may appeal to Voters, but suggesting a 'chest-
thumping, bull in the China Shop' diplomacy - whether he knows it
or not - would be utterly counterproductive, especially with a proud
culture where 'saving face' can still become the paramount issue to
the detriment of our overall objective.[87] And, although Trump would
like to think he was the first to criticize President Obama (as well as
Presidents Bush (43) and Clinton) for being too deferential to China,
this very issue was raised by this author – in a less visceral manner
- two years earlier in 2009 (*What Obama and the Democrats Knew
that McCain Didn't* - Copyright 2009 – Pages 191-194). Specifically:

> **Given the current level of China exports of goods to the
> U.S. over the past ten years, the government of China and**

its economy is - and will increasingly become – dependent on our country's continued acceptance of its exports from and commerce with China…Regrettably, though, over the past two decades, there has been a reluctance, concern and, quite frankly, timidity, in 'playing hardball' with China on the issue of trade (by both the Clinton and Bush Administrations). Moreover, our lack of resolve in even discussing the trade issue, as a 'bargaining chip' with China, over the years, will continue to be perceived by China as appeasement and, thus weakness on the part of the United States.

The truth be told: Although patient, China truly does expect to, one day, rule the world. And, candidly, in the meantime the primary foreign policy objective of both China and Russia is to foment challenges and roadblocks to U.S. foreign policy initiatives throughout the world whenever and wherever they can (colloquially stated: 'Pulling our Chain'). And as much as President Obama and the Democrats would like to hope, neither government can be trusted nor is either government our friend.

That doesn't mean that they have to be our enemies. **But, from the perspective of China and Russia, by naively believing he can, one day, 'win them over' as friends, President Obama is perceived by both countries as showing weakness and vulnerability to being manipulated,** and, as such, is only emboldening both China and Russia, in negotiating, to 'drive an even harder bargain' and hold out even longer (especially, if there's a Mid-Term or Presidential Election approaching).

Understand that the Communist China Government is not

immoral, but 'amoral;' meaning that China's Supremacy is paramount where the 'ends justify the means' (i.e. whatever they can get away with) and, never what's morally 'right' from our perspective. And, left unchallenged, they'll just keep pushing the envelope on all fronts.

Like during the holidays, in 2007, when the government in China wouldn't allow U.S. ships, with Servicemen's families aboard, to dock in China for some still unknown reason. What 'pushback' or penalty was China ever made to pay for such ridiculous/childish diplomatic behavior? None - not even an apology. But rather than confrontation, **when there's virtually no 'pushback' (neither economically nor diplomatically) by the U.S. on anything, it only encourages the government of China - which interprets our timidity as appeasement and weakness** (like China's 'Paper Tiger' label of the U.S. in the 1950s and '60s) - to keep on pressing relentlessly while, incidentally, China continues an exponential build-up of its own military.

The Trade issue is our only 'hammer' to gain cooperation from China; but it's only a 'hammer' if we dare to use it.

The Folly of 'Going into Battle Unarmed'

The truth be told, the glaring metaphor for just how economically beholden the Obama Administration perceives it is to China, is it inexplicably holds a State Dinner (in 2009) for a leader and a country that has no compunction about nor has ever apologized for or intends to stop:

1. Continued attempts of theft of American intellectual property;

2. Constant espionage attempts hoping to gain U.S. military secrets;

3. Impenetrable China import trade barriers to U.S. products;

4. Confirmed attempts to probe and disrupt U.S. internet capability (i.e. cyber- attacks);

5. While China refuses to allow its own countryman (Liu Xiaobo) to accept the Nobel Peace Prize for Freedom because he is currently being jailed for his pro-democracy activities.

But, for Trump to propose confronting China, in a big way, on the reciprocal trade issue armed with nothing more than bluster is short-sighted. Especially when China could be 'disarmed economically' first.

Eliminate China's Economic Stranglehold on the U.S. National Debt: The Issuance of 'Economic War Bonds'

Prior to confronting China in private diplomacy, with the 'option' - rather than an 'ultimatum' - to either 1) stop devaluing their currency or 2) face the public imposition of a commensurate tariff on imports from China into the United States, it would seem more prudent that the President first prepare himself and the country to deal from a position of strength. **Specifically, prior to boldly, but diplomatically, confronting China (in private) on this issue, why not, through the Federal Reserve, initiate a one-time offering to American Taxpayers** - rather than to Ben Bernanke's favored Member

Banks - of a Treasury Bond issue equal to the amount owed to China currently estimated at $900+ Billion (Now, in 2015, $1.3 Trillion).

Why shouldn't the average American, for once, be allowed in 'on the gravy train' that has been available, for the past (now six) years, to only the Big Banks, other Federal Reserve member banks and Corporate America, engineered by Ben Bernanke (with the blessing of Barack Obama) in the wake of the 2008 Economic Meltdown, which ultimately propelled those Big Banks to record profit's the very next year? Rather than banks, this time the American People could first be offered the same generous 'above-market' 3% yield offered to the Big Banks - but make it tax-free interest income as well (as opposed to taxable interest income which would only amount to an after-tax yield of 2 ¼%; assuming a 25% tax rate). At a 3% tax-free yield, the American People would clearly benefit economically and it would prove to be an immensely popular investment vehicle for the average American.

However, how this would specifically benefit the United States in its dealing with China, those funds raised through this one-time Treasury offering should be earmarked and segregated as a reserve and available as insurance only for the purpose of 'covering' the redemption or threat of redemption, by China, of their current holdings of U.S. debt. Armed with this "economic weapon," then confront China, diplomatically; on its unjust manipulation of its own currency and let them decide which way they want to go (i.e. either stop the currency manipulation or suffer the public imposition of a commensurate tariff) - but not before.

Secondly, and just as important, diplomatically inform China that, unless all Cyber-attacks, all Intellectual Theft, and all National Security espionage by China against the United States ends now and forever, a separate and additional 25% tariff will forever be imposed on China imports. Such continued behavior on their part isn't a game – it is war.

The obvious and unspoken concern is that such an ultimatum could precipitate a trade war or – worse yet – potentially re-ignite the decades-old issue of Taiwan/Formosan Sovereignty. However, the economic risk or 'point of no return' has long-since passed and China will not cease and desist unless called out. Although, the bet is that, in actuality, the government in China has more to fear from how it will economically placate a populace of 1.3 Billion in need of keeping their jobs (if suddenly decimated by debilitating American tariffs) than having to discontinue its ability to brazenly push the espionage envelope or considering annexing Taiwan in spite."

3. The Iran Nuclear Deal: Obama and the U.N. "Trashing" the Nuclear Non-Proliferation Treaty

As late as January 2013, U.N. Secretary-General Ban Ki-moon reiterated that Iran must live up to its previously long-standing signed commitment never to develop nuclear weapons:

> *"I am deeply concerned about Iran's nuclear program. I visited Iran last August and emphatically urged the country's leaders to take concrete steps to reassure the world community about the exclusive nature of its nuclear program.*[88]

As to the United Nations Nuclear Non-Proliferation Treaty of which Iran is a signatory, in September 2009 before the United Nations, President Obama similarly made his position emphatically clear, endorsing U.N. policy at that time:

1. *"First, we must stop the spread of nuclear weapons and seek the goal of a world without them...and those nations without [nuclear weapons, like Iran] have the responsibility to forsake them...Those nations that refuse to live up to their obligations must face consequences."*

2. *"[This] is about standing up for the rights of all nations that do live up to their responsibilities.* ***Because a world in which IAEA inspections are avoided and the U.N. demands are ignored will leave all people less safe and all nations less secure."***

3. ***"If they put nuclear weapons ahead of regional stability...then they must be held accountable. The world must stand together to demonstrate that international law is not an empty promise, and that treaties will be enforced."***

However, regarding the April 2015 tentative deal struck by President Obama, in a public "about face" United Nations Secretary-General Ban Ki-moon immediately endorsed the plan, stating that it *"would provide for substantial limits on Iran's nuclear program and the removal of all sanctions."*[89] Thus, it was no surprise when the U.N. Security Council subsequently approved the final Iran Nuclear Deal unanimously in July 2015. Further, given that the vote in the Security Council was unanimous, note that the deal negotiated by President Obama simultaneously met and placated the geopolitical desires and interests of Russia and China, as both staunch allies of Iran and permanent members of the Security Council.

Ultimately, it does make one wonder who originally was really "driving the bus" on the nuclear weapons deal with Iran – President Obama or U.N. Secretary-General Ban Ki-moon. Secondly, when in time did both men abruptly change their minds, relenting to Iran's insistence to, one day, obtain nuclear weapons capability?

Although both men had a common goal: To resolve the Iran Nuclear issue before each man left their respective office by the end of 2016. Odds are that it has been a joint effort and a meeting of the minds by both men to, in effect; invalidate the 45-year-old Nuclear Non-proliferation Agreement by - for the first time – allowing a non-nuclear State signatory (i.e. Iran) to ultimately go ahead anyway and, in 10 to 15 years, legally obtain nuclear weapons. An unprecedented 180 degree change and withdrawal of the publically-stated positions of both Barack Obama and Ban Ki-moon that only occurred sometime within just the last year (sometime after May 2014) before reaching a deal in April 2015.

You can now tear up the 45-year old Non-Proliferation Treaty. No longer is there anything that can bind any of the other remaining 181 non-nuclear signatory nations once even one such nation is granted a special dispensation.

Nevertheless, once again, Barack Obama, in concert with and doing the bidding of the United Nations, has worked his will - above and in contradiction to the will of a decided majority of the American People. Moreover, whether Congress could have overrode a Presidential veto of the Iran deal or not is immaterial, in that Mr. Obama knows he has already effectively won - once the

United Nations economic sanctions are ultimately repealed as a consequence of the U.N.'s unanimous approval of the deal in July 2015.

The Agreement Details

Specifically, the tentative deal struck with Iran would effectively postpone its weapons-grade nuclear uranium enrichment program for a period of 10-15 years. Yet, since at least 2008, Barack Obama – in no uncertain terms – has stated on no less than 28 separate occasions that, under no circumstances would he ever allow Iran to obtain nuclear weapons; beginning in 2008 during the second Presidential Debate:

> *"We cannot allow Iran to get a nuclear weapon. It would be a game-changer in the Region...And so it's unacceptable. And I will do everything that's required to prevent it."*

Just as significant, only two months prior to the American People going to the polls in the 2012 Presidential Election, in September 2012 at the United Nations annual meeting of world leaders, President Obama reiterated, *"Make no mistake: A nuclear-armed Iran is not a challenge to [just] be contained...The United States will do what we must to prevent Iran from obtaining a nuclear weapon."* Could President Obama sound anymore adamant about his resolve to prevent Iran from ever getting a nuclear weapon?

Albeit an obviously untrue statement today, two months before the 2012 Presidential election, President Obama's "reassurance" to the American People that Iran would never be allowed to have a nuclear weapon, *politically,* put that particular major foreign policy issue to rest for good in getting him passed his re-election. Moreover, even a year later (September 2013) at the United Nations, "Obama made clear in his morning remarks that the United States was committed to preventing Iran from developing a nuclear weapon: *'We will not tolerate the development or use of weapons of mass destruction.'* "[90]

Obama Demonizes his Opposition

Nevertheless, in August 2015, President Obama set out to demonize all Republicans and Conservatives in Congress who dared to oppose the final deal he ultimately struck with Iran that, indeed, *will guarantee* Iran's legal right to possess nuclear weapons in as early as 10-15 years:

> *"It's those Iranian hardliners chanting "Death to America" who have been most opposed to the deal. They're making common cause with the Republican caucus."*
> President Barack Obama – The American University – June 5, 2015

However, even noted liberal journalists sympathetic to the Obama Administration, like Mark Halperin and the Washington Post's Charles Lane, both admonished President Obama indicating that, if his purpose was to appear politically non-confrontational in hopes of truly building a consensus for his Iran Nuclear Deal, his speech at the American University that day was *not* Mr. Obama's finest hour.

The unadulterated partisanship of President Obama, in equating Congressional Republicans with Iranian hardliners (which presumably must even include their leader Ayatollah Khamenei as well) was, indeed, unbecoming of the office he holds. To be specific, President Obama's vailed ridicule and intolerance of those holding opposing viewpoints on display at the American University that day is born of audacity and an imperious attitude built upon and reminiscent of previous occasions when he has chosen to deride Republicans by reminding (i.e. gloating) that he won both Presidential Elections. Although again, lest he and we not forget that President Obama would have otherwise *actually lost* the 2012 Presidential Election (according to independent opinion polls – Chapter 1) if he hadn't consciously chosen to dupe the American People by lying to them (according to non-partisan *Politifact*) about ObamaCare.

Finally, consider the astonishing hypocrisy in that, as recently as May 2014 just one year earlier, President Obama, himself, publically held the exact same position as those Republicans in Congress that he is now castigating (i.e. in opposition to Iran ever being allowed to possess nuclear weapons):

> *"[W]e reserve all options to prevent Iran from obtaining nuclear weapons."*
> President Barack Obama – West Point – May 28, 2014

But now in hailing the April 2015 tentative deal, President Obama insisted that it *"would shut down Iran's path to a [nuclear] bomb from either uranium or plutonium."*[91] However, regarding the tentative agreement struck with Iran, it doesn't "shutdown," but only postpones the weapons-grade uranium enrichment for a period of 10-15 years.

Further, although knowing that it most probably won't affect him, President Obama was quick to stress that no future President of the United States would be precluded from acting – even militarily - against Iran if it is found to have violated or renounced its adherence to the agreement. Nonetheless, according to the terms of the agreement, President Obama, along with the United Nations, is still effectively and legally sanctioning Iran's right to have nuclear weapons once the 10-15 year period has past – so long as Iran adheres to the terms of the deal.

According to President Obama, the deal *"would insure that Iran could not race for a [nuclear] bomb for at least a decade – and would establish a permanent inspection regime to catch any cheating."*[92] However, even Mr. Obama, himself, conceded:

> *"What is a more relevant fear would be that in year 13, 14, 15, they [Iran] have advanced centrifuges that enrich uranium fairly rapidly, and at that point, the breakout times [to make a nuclear weapon] would have shrunk almost down to zero."*[93]

The Potential for a Nuclear Arms Race in the Middle East (Another Stark Contradiction)

Indeed, Barack Obama is no longer saying that Iran cannot be allowed to acquire a nuclear weapon. Rather, now Mr. Obama is only saying that Iran will not acquire nuclear weapons capability "on his watch" – i.e. during his Presidency. Second, **President Obama is now contradicting prior statements (made as recently as 2012) that, for Iran to possess a nuclear weapon would potentially destabilize and trigger a nuclear arms race in the Middle East region and, therefore would be "unacceptable."**

> *"Make no mistake: A nuclear-armed Iran...risks triggering a nuclear-arms race in the [Middle East] region, and the unraveling of the Non-Proliferation treaty."*
> President Barack Obama –At the United Nations – September 25, 2012

Although now Mr. Obama contradicts himself again, saying (in getting a nuclear arms deal with Iran) that there is no evidence that such an arms race would ensue after all because the neighboring countries in the region would – he believes – opt for and be satisfied with assurances from the United States that it would protect them (i.e. come under the "nuclear umbrella" of the United States). Rather than each country feeling compelled to separately develop their own nuclear weapons programs and arsenal.[94] As to Mr. Obama's stated concern that a potential arms race in the region could trigger "the unraveling of the Non-Proliferation treaty," critics would say that is precisely what the 2015 Iran Nuclear Deal struck by Obama has already accomplished.

However, it has been widely reported that the neighboring adversarial Arab nations to Iran - i.e. Saudi Arabia, Egypt, United Arab Emirates, Qatar, Kuwait, Bahrain and Oman – are poised to start their own nuclear weapons programs regardless of any nuclear deal struck by Mr. Obama. As a demonstration of their suspicions and lack of enthusiasm about the Iran Nuclear deal, other than the leaders from Bahrain and Oman, four other Arab country leaders (including Saudi Arabia) declined to even attend the May 2015 summit, in Washington DC, called for by President Obama. Ostensibly, "the Obama Administration planned the summit as a way to build Arab support for the (April 2015 tentative) Iran Nuclear Deal by giving them more arms and security guarantees to members of the six-nation Gulf Cooperation Council."[95]

The President had hoped to persuade all six leaders of the Gulf Cooperation Council to accept nuclear "umbrella" protection from the United States in lieu of developing their own nuclear weapons programs (i.e. to prevent a regional arms race). But, the Arab nations are balking – unimpressed by the announced terms thus far publicized in the tentative nuclear deal struck with Iran in April 2015.

The collective concerns of these predominantly Sunni-led nations in the Middle East that have historically been allied with the United States over the last forty years have also been exacerbated by a concerted effort of President Obama to appear – not so much as an ally – but more of a neutral observer in the region for the overriding purpose of further assuaging Iran. However, noted foreign policy expert Ian Bremmer (The Eurasia Group) has termed President Obama's intention to appear as instead a *"deeply concerned"* neutral broker in the Middle East as the *"'Ban Ki moon-ization' of U.S. foreign policy."* Similarly, Congressman Ed Royce, Chairman of the U.S. House Foreign Affairs Committee believes *"[T]he perception in the [Middle East] region is that [the United States] is tilting toward Iran"* (MSNBC - Morning Joe - 1/ 5/2016).

Taking Heed of "Security Assurances" Previously Made to Ukraine

However, remember: One need only look at the 2014 permanent incursion by Russia into eastern Ukraine and the annexation of Crimea to understand why the six Arab nations and Egypt remain skeptical of any proposed U.S. "nuclear umbrella" guarantee. Indeed, how has that worked out thus far for Ukraine as a sovereign nation?

To wit, regarding Ukraine, in a 1994 international agreement, Ukraine gave up, at the time, the third-largest nuclear arsenal in the world in exchange for so-called guaranteed "Security Assurances." Specifically, according to the 1994 "Budapest Memorandum of Security Assurance," the United States, United Kingdom and, more to the point, Russia "agreed to respect the independence and sovereignty and the existing borders of Ukraine [and] reaffirm their obligation to refrain from threat or use of force against the territorial integrity or political independence of Ukraine." However, given that A) no country – most notably the United States - has come to Ukraine's requested military aid thus far and B) eastern Ukraine, including annexed Crimea, remains occupied indefinitely almost two years later, the Budapest Memorandum rings hollow and the Gulf Cooperation Council of Arab nations may be wise to take note, assuming they haven't already.

Iranian Objections to the Deal

However, one would have thought that the 2015 Iran Nuclear Deal was hardly done. In particular, subsequent to the announcement of a tentative deal on April 2, 2015, the Iranian President Hassan Rouhani, but more importantly, the Iranian Supreme Leader Ayatollah Khamenei adamantly denounced the following crucial terms of the tentative deal – any one of which unresolved should, in theory, have doom it to failure:

1. Iran will, under no circumstances, agree to unannounced immediate inspections of suspected nuclear weapons sites;

2. Iran will not allow the inspection of any military sites for evidence of nuclear weapons development and

3. All economic sanctions currently imposed by the United Nations, in addition to those separately imposed by the United States, must be lifted on "Day One" of the implementation of the agreement - and not gradually over time until all terms of the deal have been met by the Iranians.

4. Further "rubbing the United States' nose in it," in clear defiance of world opinion, Iran continues undeterred - performing ballistic missile tests in violation of U.N. Security Council resolutions prohibiting such action (i.e. October and November 2015 – just months after agreeing to the Iran nuclear deal).

And none of the potential roadblocks listed above – any one of which alone should, as announced, ultimately have been a deal-breaker – even begins to address the largest of them all: The extent to which Iraq will, in practice, attempt to block an effective verification regime "on the ground" once the agreement is implemented. **Yet, it was obvious to most everyone – not the least of which, the Iranians – that President Obama, as a legacy achievement, was desperate to consummate a nuclear agreement; almost any agreement with the Iranians that Iran would agree, on paper, to postpone their nuclear ambitions for at least ten years.** Notwithstanding that the "anytime/anywhere" inspection stipulation listed above was previously deemed as irrevocable by the Obama Administration and the State Department just three months prior to the July 2015 finalized deal, as follows:

1. *"Well, Jake [Tapper - CNN] first of all, under this deal, you will have 'anytime, anywhere' access."*
Ben Rhodes, National Security Advisor to President Obama – April 6, 2015

2. *"We expect to have 'anywhere, anytime' access."*
Ernest Moniz, Secretary of Energy, Nuclear Physicist and chief Iran Nuclear Deal Negotiator (second in authority only to Secretary of State John Kerry) – April 18, 2015

But, on July 19, 2015, just three months later (with Energy Secretary Moniz sitting right next to him), Secretary of State John Kerry countermanded the statements of both Moniz and Rhodes – advising the world that *a 24-day waiting period* would now be permissible; contending that any violation committed by the Iranians could not be covered up in less than 3 ½ weeks' time:

> *"The fact is that in arms-control, there is no country anywhere on this planet that has 'anywhere, anytime.' There is no such standard in arms-control inspections* [as immediate 'anywhere, anytime' inspections]."
> John Kerry, U.S. Secretary of State – *Fox News Sunday* - July 19, 2015.

Just as significant, there are four known major nuclear enrichment facilities in Iran at Natanz, Fahan, Arak and Fordow. Of particular note, the Fordow site is, according to Iran, a military site. Moreover, it is the only one of the four sites that is impenetrable from any aerial bomber attack – having been constructed deep underground precisely to withstand such an attack. However, it is the Iranian position that, since it has agreed to dismantle its nuclear enrichment capabilities at Fordow, it would then constitute solely a military site and, thus now and forever be off limits to U.N. inspectors.

Consequently, the "anywhere, anytime" argument is to a large degree irrelevant now as, according to the July 2015 final agreement, all military facilities are "off limits" to U.N. inspectors anyway. Now, should the Iranians choose to surreptitiously build a nuclear weapon, they would be fools not to locate it in an off-limits military site and, for good measure, use the one military site that is impregnatable to aerial attack - Fordow. Just how does the deal cut by John Kerry and Barack Obama prevent and guarantee against this scenario ever happening? Thus, there would be no way to determine whether Iran – subsequent to signing the agreement – had reconstituted its nuclear uranium processing at declared military sites banned from U.N. inspectors or not.

What's more: According to a separate, unannounced "side deal" with the International Atomic Energy Agency, Secretary Kerry – by not rejecting it outright publically – is effectively relenting yet again by conceding to allow the Iranians themselves to collect their own soil samples requested by inspectors without any means to determine A) from exactly where the samples were taken and/or B) whether the Iranians had pre-tested the samples for detection of violations before deigning to turn them over.

Critics, ranging from noted Conservatives and Republicans to Israeli Prime Minister Benjamin Netanyahu, say no deal is better than a bad deal. Whereas President Obama apparently believes that, if the best deal that can be struck is a postponement of 10-15 years before Iran gets a nuclear weapon, it is a good deal and should be taken – if, according to Obama, the only other alternative is ultimately military confrontation.

Finally, in the days leading up to the June 30, 2015 deadline for a final agreement to the April 2015 tentative nuclear deal with Iran, five former high-ranking officials in the Obama Administration (including General David Petraeus, former CIA Director, Dennis Ross, noted U.S. diplomat and treaty negotiator, and Robert Einhorn, a former member of the U.S. negotiating team with Iran) had, in a letter, seriously cautioned President Obama about finalizing this nuclear deal with Iran. Their determination was based primarily upon the preliminary agreement struck and the subsequent objections to it already raised publicly by the Iranians, who, first and foremost, refuse to allow U.N. inspectors unrestricted access to all suspected nuclear sites; including military installations. Secondly, in August 2015, at least 200 former military generals and high ranking military personnel, in a letter to President Obama similarly warned against approving the Iran Nuclear Deal as negotiated.

Woodward's Defense of Obama's Iran Deal

Probably the most ardent defense of President Obama comes from not a Democrat politician, but from renowned investigative reporter Bob Woodward. Specifically, Woodward contends, rather, that the American People owe Mr. Obama a profound debt of gratitude for taking the politically unpopular position of even attempting to negotiate the Iran Nuclear Deal he and John Kerry did with Iran.[96] Alternatively, if viewed as an audition, consciously or unconsciously, Woodward's impassioned defense of Mr. Obama did nothing either to hurt his future chances of getting exclusive access to the Oval Office just one last time to write another book about the Obama Presidency.

American People Say Iran Will Cheat Regardless

But, will Iran live up to the terms of the deal it struck with Obama? The American People – by more than a two to one margin – are not confident and/or still believe that regardless of the deal struck; the Iranians will cheat and surreptitiously build a nuclear weapon anyway:

> Consider the polling: In this month's (March 2015) NBC/ Wall Street Journal poll, 71% of respondents said they

believe a deal would not prevent the Iranians from obtaining a nuclear weapon…In a February (2015) Gallup Poll, 77% of Americans believed that Iran's development of nuclear weapons pose a "critical threat" to the United States.[97]

Lastly, based on an August 2015 Quinnipiac poll taken a month after the final Iran Nuclear Deal was struck, Voters in "swing states" passed their final decisive judgment – 59% (nearly 6 in 10) opposed to 25% (only 1 in 4) supporting the President's agreement:

	Florida	Ohio	Pennsylvania	Average
Opposed	61%	58%	61%	59%
Support	25%	24%	26%	25%
Don't Know	14%	18%	13%	16%

President Obama continues to contend that the Iran Nuclear Deal calls for the most stringent U.N. inspection regime ever negotiated. Yet, according to the IAEA side-deal, Iran inexplicably still gets to gather its own soil samples?

It is ironic and sadly naïve that both President Obama and Secretary of State John Kerry are so eager to shake hands and deal with Iran, totally ignoring when, just a few years earlier during the Iraq War, Iran was arming our enemy in Iraq with IEDs used to kill at least 500 U.S. troops and maim hundreds more, but was never made to pay any penalty for it - as if it had never happened.

2 2 2

After seven years of foreign policy dealings with Russia (on nuclear weapons reductions and the Ukraine incursion) and China (on currency manipulation, unfair trade and cyber espionage), President

Obama has been stymied and largely ineffective in compelling either country to abandon or even modify their aggressive behavior – be it through global geopolitical expansion, economic trade barriers or cyber warfare. To the contrary, throughout the Obama Presidency, the aggressive behavior of both Russia and China has, if anything only intensified.

However, the political leaders of both Russia and China view Barack Obama as weak precisely because of the image he has cultivated as being a non-confrontational peacemaker and, thus perceive President Obama as someone who would be vulnerable and prone to being manipulated in negotiations. And, although the image of a conciliatory non-confrontational peacemaker may impress at the United Nations, it is utterly counter-productive for the President of the United States in dealing with Russia and China who, historically, do not like, but grudgingly respect "push-back" from their adversaries.

Secondly, and just as disconcerting, is President Obama's vulnerability driven by Presidential legacy achievement considerations. As evidence, it was not a secret to anyone that President Obama viewed an Iran Nuclear Deal as the crowning foreign policy achievement of his Presidency. The problem: The Iranians knew it as well and, accordingly, negotiated concession after concession. Similarly, Russian President Putin knew President Obama considered the 2011 Nuclear Arms Reduction START Treaty as his number one foreign policy achievement of his first term. Consequently, it was no coincidence that, early into Russia's incursion in Ukraine, Putin saw leverage with Obama and played his trump card – making the public threat to back off Barack Obama's other considered Presidential legacy foreign policy accomplishment, the START Treaty, if further pressured by the United States to withdraw from Ukraine.

CHAPTER 8

81 *SkyNews* "Annan's Plea for a Nuclear-Free World " - May 3, 2005.

82 *Seattle Times* "White House Looking at Deep Cuts to Nukes" by Walter Pincus and Craig Whitlock – February 15, 2012.

83 Source: *The Heritage Foundation* "An Independent Assessment of New START" – Ibid - April 30, 2010.

84 Council on Foreign Relations "The Global Nuclear Non-Proliferation Regime" – Issue Brief – June 23, 2013.

85 *America at the Precipice* – Ibid - Pages 200-201.

86 *Jump-Starting Real Job Creation in America* by Gary R. Patterson (Copyright 2012) – Pages 144-151.

87 You would really like to think that Trump knows this. But then, again, given the opportunity to re-evaluate his position on Iraq, Trump, astoundingly, is apparently serious about the right of the United States to seize Iraqi oil wells until this country has recouped the hundreds of billions of dollars spent on the Iraqi War. Yeah, the Iraqis 1) are ungrateful; 2) believe they did the United States 'a favor' and 3) think they owe us nothing. We get that. But how does Trump's idea differ from Germany attempting to seize Russian oil fields in the Caucuses and Japan invading China for its raw materials during World War II?

88 *United Nations Secretary-General's Remarks at Monterey Institute of International Studies* "Advancing the Disarmament and Non-Proliferation Agenda" – January 18, 2013.

89 *McClatchy DC* "Iran Agrees Tentatively to Massive Cuts in Nuclear Capabilities; Experts Surprised" by Matthew Schofield – April 2, 2015.

90 *CNN* "Rouhani: Nuclear Weapons Have No Place in Iran's Security" by Jim Sciutto, Jennifer Rizzo and Tom Cohen – September 25, 2013.

91 *McClatchy DC* –Ibid – April 2, 2015.

92 *New York Times* "Iran's Supreme Leader Says Sanctions Must Lift When Nuclear Deal is Signed" by Thomas Erdbrink and David E. Sanger – April 9, 2015.

93 *National Public Radio* – Interview with President Barack Obama – April 7, 2015.

94 *The Atlantic* " 'Look… It's My Name on this': Obama Defends the Nuclear Deal" by Jeffrey Goldberg – May 21, 2015.

95 *Wall Street Journal* "Rulers Snub Arab Summit, Clouding U.S. Bid for Iran Deal" by Jay Solomon, Carol E. Lee and Ahmed Al Omran – May 11, 2015.

96 *MSNBC Morning Joe* – August 19, 2015.

97 *National Journal* "On Iran, Obama Is Ignoring Public Opinion at His Own Peril" by Josh Kraushaar - March 19, 2015.

Article 51 of the U.N. Charter and other Decisions Exemplifying Obama's Commitment to U.N. Multinational Policy

1. **Cuba: The Joint United Nations' Demand and Barack Obama's Intent to End the 54-Year Trade Embargo**

    "The General Assembly today adopted a resolution which for the 23rd year in a row called for an end to the United States' economic, commercial and financial embargo on Cuba.

    "Exposing an intractable demarcation of the international community, 188 Member States voted in favour and, as in previous years, the United States and Israel voted against... (The U.N.) once again urged States that had continued to apply such laws repeal and invalidate them as soon as possible, in line with their obligations under the United Nations Charter and international law."

    United Nations – Meetings Coverage and Press Release – October 28, 2014

"We will end an approach that for decades has failed to advance [U.S.] interests and instead will begin to normalize relations between our two countries. These 50 years have shown that isolation has not worked. It's time for a new approach."
President Barack Obama – Two months later, announcing his intention that the United States initiate formal diplomatic relations with Cuba – December 17, 2014

The principal purpose of this discussion is not whether it is advisable for the United States to re-establish formal diplomatic relations with Cuba, now or in the future. Rather, the focus is to further illustrate yet another major United Nations foreign policy position which President Obama has embraced whole-heartedly and is in lockstep agreement: The 23-year-old United Nations' emphatic and diametric opposition to the trade embargo that the United States has imposed against Cuba for now over a half a century.

It should be noted that, as far back as his 2008 Presidential Election bid, Barack Obama had publically endorsed opening up formal diplomatic relations with Cuba. Although, Mr. Obama was again preceded (i.e. not an original idea of his own) on still another major foreign policy position that had already been originally adopted by the United Nations 17 years earlier (1991).

"Obama is using Executive Authority – the best friend of a second-term president facing a hostile Congress – to establish diplomatic relations with Cuba for the first time since 1961." However, ultimately, it is only within the purview of Congress to sanction lifting the trade embargo.[98]

Pre-conditions Sought by the American People before Lifting the Embargo

In recent years there has been a dramatic shift in the percentage of Americans who support re-establishing diplomatic relations with Cuba. **Although, digging deeper into the data, a majority of the American People still oppose the idea, unless it is first accompanied by a commitment from the Cuban government to begin holding free elections and a move towards a free market economy. However, to date, Cuba has agreed to neither of these pre-conditions as held by a majority of the American People:**

> Those polled, however, said they were concerned about Cuba's human rights record under Fidel Castro and remain concerned now that Castro's brother, Raul, is running the country. Fifty percent of those surveyed nationally view Castro's repression of political dissent as a reason to keep the current policy (of imposing a trade embargo…Further) most of those polled, except Latinos, said they see the continuation of the Castro regime as a reason to keep the current (Trade Embargo) policy…[99]

Illustrative of just how politically-charged the Cuban Trade Embargo issue is, 2016 Republican Presidential Candidate Marco Rubio vehemently protested President Obama's Executive Action:

> *"This entire policy is based on an illusion, on a lie, the lie and the illusion that more commerce and access to money and goods will translate into political freedom for the Cuban people. All this is going to do is give the Castro regime, which controls every aspect of Cuban life, the opportunity to manipulate these changes to perpetuate itself in power."*[100]

Exemplifying the degree to which the Castro regime still maintains its repressive grip on the Cuban people in the 21st century, to further suppress freedom of thought or dissent, the Cuban Government still does not permit unfettered access to the internet by its people.

Pulling out all the stops on the same day of his announcement, President Obama formally and publically thanked Pope Francis for his support of Obama's Cuba rapprochement initiative:

> *"I want to thank his Holiness Pope Francis, whose moral example shows us the importance of pursuing the world as it should be, rather than simply settling for the world as it is."*

Although, four months earlier (August 2014), President Obama chose not to publically accept the advice and endorsement of Pope Francis on an event of even more immediate importance: Specifically, the belief of Pope Francis is that the international community is justified in using whatever level of force is necessary for the immediate protection of tens of thousands of Christians still being persecuted by the Islamic State, which has already murdered countless numbers of Christians thus far.

Finally, while still President, it would not be surprising at all for Barack Obama to triumphantly visit Cuba to allow himself to be lauded by the Cuban people.

2. Obama's Distain and Avoidance of World War II and Cold War Era Commemorations and Why

The 70th Anniversary of Victory in Europe Day (May 8, 2015)

Was President Obama's scheduled absence at 1) the May 8th 2015

70th Anniversary of Victory in Europe Day (V-E Day), held in his home of Washington DC and 2) the November 2009 Commemoration of the 20th Anniversary of the Triumphant End to the Cold War, held in Berlin, Germany (see Chapter 2) a conscious reflection of his concern that such commemorations wrongly emphasize and laud the prior success and victories of superpower nations over evil - at the expense of Mr. Obama's preference for the United Nations Multinational model for resolving global conflict today? Therefore in President Obama's mind, such commemorations should not be encouraged or extolled?

> (The 70th Anniversary of V-E Day was meant) to honor the heroes who fought in (World War II) and those on the home front who produced the tanks, ships and aircraft that enabled the United States and its Allies to achieve victory…As part of a thrilling three-day celebration in the nation's capital, the May 8 event will also coincide with a ceremony for Veterans at the World War II National Memorial.

> *"From time to time, we need to remind ourselves just how much we have accomplished as a nation. May 8th 2015 Arsenal of Democracy Flyover in Washington DC will provide us with exactly that opportunity – a chance to recognize those men and women who made the sacrifices necessary to preserve freedom here at home and around the world, a moment in time to reflect on the awesome power of this country and its people when we focus on a common goal."*
> John Cudahy, President, International Council of Air Shows – February 4, 2015[101]

However, on April 13, 2015 – less than a month before the celebration of the 70th Anniversary of V-E Day in Washington DC

was to occur on May 8, 2015, it was announced that, instead, President Barack Obama would be making a junior college commencement speech at Lake Area Technical Institute, in Watertown, South Dakota. Note that at least since February 4, 2015 – clearly two months earlier than that – the announcement of the Washington DC celebration of V-E Day had already been made public. Yet, President Obama chose – as a higher priority in his mind - to be elsewhere than attending this momentous Washington DC World War II commemoration ceremony.

Although no one in the media was apparently curious enough to have ever ask at the time, the President's men in the Administration would presumably say that it was a higher priority – in terms of timeliness and importance - for President Obama to speak at a community college on May 8th 2015 to promote his proposal (albeit announced over three months earlier) to pay for two years' free college tuition for everyone at all junior colleges nationwide. Further, his people might also note that on the previous day, the President was in Oregon visiting Nike Headquarters promoting his trade bill.

Presumably, neither the President nor his political handlers would attempt to further buttress the priority importance of being out of town on May 8th 2015 by touting the President's necessity for also attending a fund raiser the night before. More to the point, did President Obama or his political operatives – who are all about maximizing image and press coverage – think that a junior college commencement speech in South Dakota that day would somehow have been able to compete with and garner more coverage than Mr. Obama would have gotten, alternatively appearing at the 70th Anniversary of V-E Day commemoration ceremonies at home in Washington DC? Perhaps, however, the incremental press coverage and photo "ops" of his presence at the 70th Anniversary of V-E Day celebrations would not have been the type of political coverage President Obama and his people would have wanted memorialized on the internet.

Instead, President Obama sent National Security Advisor Susan Rice to the V-E commemoration in Washington DC – opting only for a Saturday morning radio "shout-out" announcement to World War II Veterans (thus, assuring no chance for any onsite photo op).

Moreover, please note that the President's two stops the day before in Oregon were add-on events that were not even announced until late April – *two weeks after* the initial scheduling announcement on April 13, 2015 of his May 8th college commencement speech. **Consequently, President Obama clearly had at least two months' prior notice of the Washington DC 70th Anniversary V-E Day historic commemoration event occurring on May 8th – but purposely chose, alternatively to attend a college commencement in South Dakota instead.**

Does President Obama want the American People to believe that any or all of the three events that he subsequently scheduled and attended in Oregon and South Dakota for May 7-8 were anywhere near as important as his presence - as President of the United States – would have been in Washington DC on May 8th attending the 70th Anniversary of Victory in Europe Day and honoring World War II veterans? And don't try to tell the American People that the college would not have changed its commencement date to either the day before or the day after May 8th to somehow have accommodated the President of the United States as its commencement speaker.

The importance of those three events he later chose as a higher priority in his mind to attend sadly pales by comparison. Unless for

some other reason known only to him, either the President, purposely, did not prefer to attend the celebration in Washington DC and/
or saw his presence at the event, perhaps, sending the wrong signal
– being perceived, again, as highlighting American Exceptionalism
at the expense of Mr. Obama's preference for the United Nations'
Multinational worldview of global governance.

Lastly, President Obama returned from his community college commencement speech at 9:30 pm that Friday Evening on May 8th. As
part of the three-day event, however, there still were proceedings
occurring the following day - Saturday May 9, 2015 - that President
Obama, now being back in town, could have attended. But there is
no public record that he left the White House to do so.

3.   Obama's Blind Obedience to Article 51 of the United Nations Charter (The Obama Doctrine of "Leading From Behind")

As previously noted, Article 51 of the United Nations Charter precludes the United States (or any nation) from proactively launching
a military strike against another nation unless A) it is determined
to be in self-defense or B) prior approval has been granted by the
United Nations Security Council. If neither condition is met, to
launch any military strike by one nation against another is a violation of international law.

However, so long as a nation hostile to the United States (e.g. North
Korea, Iran, Syria and even Venezuela) is an ally of Russia and/or
China - who as permanent members of the Security Council have the
ability to exercise veto power over any Security Council resolution
- in essence, that hostile country comes under their protective security umbrella. Secondly complicating matters, such blind obedience to
Article 51 and submissiveness to the dominant role and authority of the

United Nations in world affairs (i.e. The Obama Doctrine of "Leading from Behind") calls into question whether President Obama therefore believes that the United States also relinquishes its right to exercise First-Strike capability (i.e. the element of surprise) in exigent circumstances - even when the United States has unilaterally determined for itself that its National Security and/or that of an ally is at stake.

Consequently, as unsuccessfully demonstrated thus far in Syria, President Obama's strict interpretation and adherence to Article 51 leaves him powerless to directly act militarily against any government in power that he may deem hostile to its citizens – other than to provide protective/defensive arms, supplies, No-Fly Zones, etc. Given such a constricted U.S. foreign policy that self-imposes upon the United States a subservient role to the dictates of the United Nations; consider the dire implications and ramifications relating to other potential "hot spots" around the globe – any one or more of which could explode in the next few years:

> **A. North Korea – What if** United States Intelligence agencies detected - with 90% certainty - that North Korea currently has operational ICBMs with nuclear-tipped warheads on a launch pad. Yet, until launched, the target country destination cannot be discerned. Given such a circumstance, would a pre-emptive military strike restricted only to surgically "taking out" those missiles constitute self-defense (on behalf of not just the U.S. but, more geographically vulnerable South Korea, Japan or any other nation in the area with whom the U.S. has a mutual defense pact); making such a strike permissible under Article 51 of the U.N. Charter without the prior approval by the Security Council? Note that although United Nations resolutions clearly prohibit North Korea from even testing ballistic missiles capable of delivering nuclear warheads, it has done

so as recently as December of 2015 - landing one within 1,500 yards of U.S. vessels in international waters.

1. Without knowing North Korea's intention until a missile is launched and a target nation, if any is discerned, is the definition and condition of "self-defense" unequivocally met under Article 51 once the nuclear-tipped warhead is "married" to the ICBM on a launch pad (as was the case during the 1962 Cuban Missile Crisis)?

2. Even if the U.N. Secretary-General and all other members of the Security Council agree, Russia and/or China could disagree as to the "certainty" of U.S. intelligence and use this as a pretext to arbitrarily veto any Security Council resolution authorizing a military strike prior to missile launch.

3. Moreover, after having approached the Security Council, the U.S. and those nations they would be acting on behalf of would necessarily be "tipping their hand" as to the element of surprise – once Russia and/or China are apprised.

4. **A further complicating factor:** Should the U.S. approach the Security Council with their 90% intelligence assurance that ICBMs are A) on a North Korean launch pad and B) armed with nuclear-tipped warheads, what if, not just Russia and/or China object – but U.N. Secretary-General Ban Ki-moon *remains unconvinced* as to the validity of the U.S. intelligence report as a pre-condition for approving a pre-emptive defensive military strike. Remember that the U.N. was 1) against the 2003 Iraq

War and its "Failure of Intelligence" and more recently in 2013 2) against a punitive military strike against Syria because U.N. Secretary-General Ban Ki-moon remained unconvinced of the 90% intelligence assurance assessment by the U.S. as to the Syrian government's responsibility for a chemical attack that killed at least 1,400 people.

If, as in Syria in 2013, President Obama believes that the United States is subservient to the authority and approval of the U.N. Secretary-General, then, in effect, would he also relinquish U.S. authority and approval for unilaterally determining First-Strike military capability in not only conventional but nuclear warfare as well? It is one thing for Barack Obama to kowtow to the U.N. and retreat from his 2013 "red line" punitive military strike threat against Syria (notwithstanding the significant loss to U.S. credibility and prestige worldwide), but does the United States ever want to surrender to the United Nations its final authority to determine for itself the National Security implications as to whether First-Strike capability – be it conventional or nuclear – is warranted or not?

Barack Obama has never been confronted with such a dire scenario thus far (as this hypothetical North Korean scenario presented herein) in his seven years as President and, hopefully, will not in his final year. But shouldn't the American People want to know where he would stand in the aforementioned scenario? Before President Obama, the United States has never before even considered "handing over" to the U.N. its right to unilaterally make the determination as to when First-Strike military action is warranted. Yet, given the aforementioned scenario and a strict interpretation of and Barack Obama's adherence to Article 51 of the U.N Charter, he would be in violation of international law to unilaterally approve such military action.

But does anyone know what he would do? Does Barack Obama know what he would do? All that is known is that the one time that President Obama was confronted with a comparable scenario with the use by Syria of chemical weapons in 2013, he blinked and retreated – withdrawing his "red line" ultimatum rather than, according to the United Nations, breaking international law (even though it has been documented that Syria has continued to use chemical weapons and chlorine gas since - in violation of international law).

And during the 2016 Presidential Campaign, the 2016 Republican nominee must be prepared to confront the Democrat nominee as well on this very issue of whether U.S. foreign policy will continue to assume a subservient role to the United Nations in matters exclusive to the best National Security interests of the American people and their allies. It would then be rightly within the purview of the American People to ultimately judge for themselves what is in their best National Security interests *before* the Election and vote accordingly.

B. Israel and Iran: The Potential for Confrontation as early as 2016

Given the 2015 Iran Nuclear Deal negotiated by President Obama, acting on behalf of the United Nations the President has effectively taken "the bat out of the hands" of Israel should their government see the necessity to attack Iran for the purpose of destroying its ability to create a nuclear weapons arsenal that threatens their National Security and, thus the existence of the state of Israel. Secondly, at least through the remainder of President Obama's second term that ends on January 20, 2017, the Iran Nuclear Deal struck by President Obama precludes the United States from assisting Israel should Israel unilaterally feel it imperative that it act against Iran before then, unless it is proven that the Iranians have violated the agreement.

In particular, logistically the military cooperation of the United States would be integral to the practical success of effectively destroying and/or substantially diminishing (set backing/postponing by years) the ability of Iran to then reconstitute a nuclear weapons program and arsenal. However, given the adoption of the Iran Nuclear Deal by both the United Nations and the United States in particular, the option of U.S. military support in any capacity for such a military attack by Israel against Iran is "off the table" at least until Barack Obama is no longer President and, only then, if his successor renounces the Deal.

As a consequence of the Iran Nuclear Deal struck and how it impacts on Israel's National Security, President Obama has arbitrarily narrowed Israel's options for them to only:

1. Option 1: Accept the Iran Nuclear Deal as negotiated by Barack Obama - in effect, abdicating to the United Nations Israel's sovereign right and responsibility to determine for itself if and when its National Security is in jeopardy of being violated (including First-Strike capability); or

2. Option 2: Wait out the final year of the Obama Presidency and hope that the Republican Party wins the 2016 Presidential Election and renounces the Iran Nuclear Deal; or

3. Option 3: Unilaterally launch a military strike against Iran if and when Israel should determine that it can no longer preclude the possibility that Iran may have already created a nuclear weapon(s) that could be used against Israel.

However, the Game-Changing Event: The Sale of S-300s to Iran by Putin

One might wonder why the Israeli government could not simply bide its time for one year to see if the Republicans do indeed take over the White House in 2017 and renounce the Iran Nuclear Deal negotiated by President Obama and approved by the United Nations (i.e. Option 2). Then, if Iran is still determined and adamant that it will not give up its nuclear enrichment capability, the United States and Israel could conceivably jointly act militarily to destroy and degrade Iran's nuclear-related capability to do so, if need be. Problem solved.

However, the problem is that, should Israel decide to wait until a new U.S. President is inaugurated, by the end of 2016 Iran most likely will already have in place and operational an anti-aircraft missile defense system with the assistance of its ally, Russia – which would effectively eliminate the possibility that Israel could destroy Iran's capacity to surreptitiously create a nuclear weapons arsenal.

Specifically, in April 2015 Russia announced its intention to sell its highly sophisticated S-300 (i.e. Almaz-Antei: S-300 PMU-1) anti-aircraft mobile missile defense system to Iran. Once operational, the only aircraft in existence that could reasonably be assured to have the capability to A) evade the S-300 anti-aircraft system and B) destroy all known potential uranium enrichment and nuclear technology-related sites in Iran is the United States' B-2 stealth bomber fleet consisting of just 20 aircraft currently.

And remember: Because the S-300 is a *mobile* system, it would be exceedingly difficult to detect and destroy. In other words, once the S-300 system is operational, there are no aircraft currently in the

Israeli air force that would have any reasonable chance of evading the anti-aircraft system and destroying all of Iran's known nuclear weapons-related sites. Consequently, once the S-300 system is operational in Iran, the option of Israel unilaterally launching a successful all-out attack on Iranian nuclear weapons-related sites is no longer viable:

> Even with the United States participating, "[A]n attack on Iran's nuclear facilities was going to be a daunting task, even under the best of circumstances, an Air Force official with extensive experience flying stealth aircraft said... The sale of the S-300 would also neutralize any possibility that Israel could take unilateral action against Iran...(The S-300) essentially makes Iran attack-proof by Israel and almost any country, without (stealth fighter) capabilities. In other words, Iran, with the S-300, can continue to do what they want once those systems are in place without fear of attack from anyone [except] the U.S. A Brilliant chess move...[102]

But Why Wouldn't President Obama Object?

Both the Department of the Defense and Israel adamantly object to and warn against the sale of the S-300 anti-aircraft missile defense system by Russia to Iran. Initially in 2007 the United States had persuaded Russia not to sell the S-300 system to Iran. Moreover, when Obama became President, his Administration extended that understanding with Russia another six years – even touting the achievement as a major foreign policy diplomatic accomplishment for President Obama.

So, one would think that, even though he may not prevail this time because of current tensions between the U.S. and Russia, President Obama would at least attempt to convince President Putin to continue his moratorium on the sale of the S-300 system to Iran. And, if unsuccessful, publically object to the deal. Right? But, if anything, President Obama seemed placidly resigned and philosophically taciturn to the prospect of S-300s in Iran – but must know full-well that, once operational the success of a unilateral military strike against Iranian nuclear sites would no longer be a viable option for Israel. Or, indeed, could that actually be President Obama's desired outcome?

> *"I'm frankly surprised that [the voluntary moratorium on the sale of the S-330 system to Iran] held this long, given that [the Russians] were not prohibited by sanctions from selling these weapons…I'm not surprised given some of the deterioration in the relationship between Russia and the United States, and the fact that [the Russian] economy is under such strain and this was a substantial sale."*
> President Barack Obama – April 17, 2015

President Obama doesn't sound that upset for something that the Obama Administration had touted for years as a major diplomatic achievement. But, why? Nary a concern expressed by President Obama as to how the S-300 system would make it appreciably more challenging – even for the United States - should it one day become necessary to "take out" Iranian nuclear sites if Iran violates or reneges on the 2015 Iran Nuclear Deal. But if so, then why was the Obama Administration so vehemently concerned as to the placement of the S-300 system in Iran for six years, yet, in 2015, it apparently is of little or no concern at all to Mr. Obama?

Once the S-300 is Operational, Israel Has No Military Option

Consequently, regarding Option 1 above, Israeli Prime Minister Netanyahu has said countless times that he would never accept or abide by the terms of the Iran Nuclear Deal if it meant relinquishing his country's sovereign right to determine their own National Security parameters and requirements for itself. So Option 1 is out. Option 2 – i.e. waiting out the 2016 Presidential Election for a GOP win and a renouncement of the Iran Nuclear Deal would be most desirable if it is reasonable to assume Iran is still at least a year away from surreptitiously creating a nuclear weapon. And should the Republicans lose in 2016, although still a "daunting task," Israel could then proceed if need be with Option 3 – a unilateral Israeli attack on Iran's nuclear sites.

However, the S-300 missile system changes all that. Specifically, if there is any possibility that Iran's S-300 anti-aircraft missile defense system becomes operational in 2016, Israel may very well decide that it does not have the luxury of time to wait for just the possibility of a GOP win. So Option 2 would be out.

Specifically, if Israel were to decide to wait out the 2016 Presidential Election and the GOP loses again (remembering that it has lost the popular vote in 5 out of the last 6 Presidential Elections), a unilateral Israeli attack on Iran's nuclear sites – Option 3 and its last option - may no longer exist as well. However, Israeli Prime Minister Netanyahu doesn't sound like the kind of guy that would *ever risk gambling away* the military option to preserve Israel's National Security.

However, in his quest to head off a military confrontation with Iran, the three options President Obama foisted upon Israel, that box Israel in, may ironically and sadly serve 1) as the catalyst for war between Iran and Israel and 2) sooner rather than later. Because, once the S-300 anti-aircraft mobile missile defense system is operational in Iran, Israel no longer has a viable conventional military option to destroy and degrade Iran's nuclear weapons capacity.

Consequently, unless 1) Israel has another unknown Stuxnet-type cyber-attack surprise designed to set back Iranian nuclear progress indefinitely or 2) intends to exercise Option 3 (i.e. a unilateral military attack on Iran nuclear sites) before the S-300 system becomes operational, Netanyahu will then have no other option than to accept the Iran Nuclear Deal. **As a consequence, guided by Article 51 of the U.N. Charter (combined with the presence of Russia's S-300 anti-aircraft defense system in Iran), President Obama, on behalf of and in deference to the dominant role and authority of the United Nations, will have worked his will once again by, in effect, disarming Israel - taking their unilateral military option "off the table" for them.** Netanyahu will thus be left with little recourse but to accept the United States and United Nations-brokered deal with Iran that will, in effect, insure Iran the legal right to possess nuclear weapons within 10-15 years.

C. Obama Administration Renounces the Monroe Doctrine

In 2013, Secretary of State John Kerry renounced the Monroe Doctrine; indicating that it was no longer viable to insure the National Defense and Security of the United States going forward. The 19th century U.S. foreign policy edict, in essence, declared that any intervention by European countries, politically or militarily, in the affairs of Western Hemisphere nations would be considered by the United States as an act of aggression. However:

> Published reports in South America say (Vladimir) Putin is seeking to create military bases in Cuba, Nicaragua, Venezuela and Argentina. All four countries are close allies of Moscow...Argentina, South America's second largest country, has agreed to host (Russian) military bases on the South American continent...Argentina and its close ally, Venezuela have long been on friendly terms with Iran. With South America in Russia's good graces, [Russia] will have a base to coordinate and store offensive weapons, putting another challenge in place for the U.S. homeland defenses...[103]

Apparently Vladimir Putin's designs on 21st century international hegemony are not confined to just the Middle East and Eastern Europe. He now perceives President Obama to be giving Russia the "green light" throughout the Western Hemisphere as well – at least until January 2017.

Yet, from President Obama's perspective, his decision to renounce the Monroe Doctrine is quite logical, given his blind acceptance to Article 51 of the U.N. Charter, which precludes any nation, including the United States, from taking either punitive or offensive military action against a nation. Unless the President was somehow certain that the U.S. would prevail in proving to the satisfaction of a majority of the United Nations Security Council, including Russia and China, that there, indeed, existed a threat to the National Security of the U.S., thus constituting a threat to its sovereignty. An unlikely circumstance.

Consequently, in Barack Obama's mind, the Monroe Doctrine stands in stark contrast and, therefore contradicts Article 51 and the preeminent role of the United Nations (as opposed to the United States) as to its exclusive and final authority to determine whether the burden of proof and tenet of "acting in self-defense" has been met. Therefore, for the United States to act unilaterally under the nearly 200-year authority of the Monroe Doctrine alone, without approval of the United Nations would be, according to U.N. Secretary-General Ban Ki moon (and, consequently, Barack Obama) a violation of international law.

However, in abandoning the Monroe Doctrine, President Obama has also surrendered the sovereign legal authority of the United States to unilaterally act against Russian military influence and dominion in the Western Hemisphere wherever and whenever Putin may chose. Finally, one wonders if, before re-establishing diplomatic relations with Cuba in 2015, whether President Obama had the presence of mind to, at least, secure a commitment from the Cuban government to renounce its agreement allowing Russia to continue with its intentions to build a military base there - just 90 miles from the United States.

4. U.N. Global Governance Versus American Exceptionalism (In the Post-World War II Real World)

To his credit, Barack Obama has mentioned on a number of occasions (including before the United Nations General Assembly), that not just the United States, but all nations must step forward and proportionately contribute military troops and assistance when called upon to support both peace-keeping and military missions throughout the world deem necessary by either the U.N. or a coalition of nations. However, this aspect of proportionate or representative participation in military support by member states of the United Nations has rarely occurred with success since the 1970s.

Although, in the case of the United Nations, early on in its 70-year history – during the Korean War and Middle East peace-keeping deployments in the 1950s and 1960s - many times U.N. forces were, indeed at the forefront. However, that has rarely been the case in recent decades because when true military conflict ensues where danger to life on a wide scale may loom; the Band-Aid of U.N. troop presence is typically withdrawn.

Consequently, in the post-World War II era that military burden has practicably and ever-increasing fallen upon the United States, by default, to undertake. Further, coalitions of nations to combat military aggression have occurred, but except for the shining example of the first Gulf War in the early 1990s, most if not all were proportionately fought by only a few countries (e.g. Britain, Canada, Australia, some European nations, etc.) with the U.S. always in the leading role.

In reality, rather than the United Nations, in the post-World War II era, it has been the military ability and might of good nations (predominantly the United States) to, if need be, stand up militarily to the aggression of bad actors and nations which has truly insured relative peace throughout the world. And although most agree that the United Nations does serve the purpose of providing at least a forum for diplomatic discussion of disputes among nations, in actuality it has ultimately been the military might of the United States in the post-World War II era that has been primarily responsible for keeping the peace worldwide - rather than the existence of the United Nations. And the world community as represented by the United Nations, at least since the 1970s has not acknowledged that fact enough.

Granting President Obama the benefit of doubt, he too understands that for the United Nations to ultimately become the dominant world body and assume true responsibility for global governance authority will require the willingness of all member states to participate militarily when called upon to meet peace-keeping challenges throughout the world. President Obama is fond of stating his belief in *"the importance of pursuing the world as it should be, rather than simply settling for the world as it is."* Although, in truth, before President Obama (and his Doctrine of "Leading from Behind"), the reality was that, in the post-World War II era, the world has counted on A) the military might of the United States "as an indispensable force for good" (i.e. American Exceptionalism) and B) the perception that the U.S. is the only nation prepared to employ it if need be, to hold aggressor nations around the world in check.

Moreover, it is difficult to envision this paradigm changing in the foreseeable future. And unless the United Nations can one day supplant the world's reliance on the United States for military defense throughout the world, the U.N. shouldn't expect to assume the dominant role in exclusive global governance anytime soon.

It is certainly not Barack Obama's fault that the United States – rather than the United Nations – has evolved to assume the role of military "policeman" throughout the world in the post-World War II era. Rather, after 70 years of collective psychological and financial dependence by the nations of the world on the United States for security and international peace, it is impossible to envision that the member states of the United Nations are now going to voluntarily assume their proportionate military role and responsibility for participating in U.N. peace-keeping missions throughout the world.

Moreover, given their 70-year dependence on the military might of the United States to always "do the right thing," today most of these nations have neither the financial resources nor military expertise themselves to establish and maintain a competent proportionate and representative fighting force if called upon. Further, because many nations never have had to devote financial resources for their individual national defense in the post-World War II era, many of these countries (as exemplified throughout Europe) over the years have fallen into the fiscal trap of diverting and overcommitting to spending excessively on social benefits programs for their people (e.g. early retirement at age 50-55, generous health benefits, vacation time, etc.). As a consequence, even if these nations wanted to, in reality because of their more than generous fiscal commitment to social programs over decades, they cannot afford now or in the foreseeable future to take on the incremental cost to build and maintain a ready fighting force to proportionately contribute militarily to the United Nations if called upon.

And that is not to affix blame. Rather, it is simply a statement of fact that has resulted as a consequence of 70 years of financial dependence on the United States to assume the military responsibility for keeping international peace. In essence, that is the practical conundrum Barack Obama, as perhaps the U.N Secretary-General one day, would have to confront and overcome. Namely, for the United Nations to ever truly achieve a greater semblance of Multinational global governance authority, it would also require that all member states of the United Nations step forward and accept their international peace-keeping military responsibility proportionately alongside the United States - rather than primarily and continually relying upon it.

CHAPTER 9

98 *MINNPOST* – "On Restoring Diplomatic Relations With Cuba: Why Obama Did It – and Why Now" by Mark Porubcansky – December 18, 2014.

99 *USAToday* "Poll: Americans Favor Normal Relations With Cuba" by Nicole Guadiano – February 2, 2014.

100 *New York Times* "U.S. to Restore Full Relations with Cuba, Erasing Last Trace of Cold War Hostility" by Peter Baker - December 19, 2014.

101 *Warbirds News* "Mega Flyover Over DC on the 70th Anniversary of VE Day" – February 4, 2015.

102 *The Daily Beast* "Putin's Missile Could Make U.S. Attack on Iran Nearly Impossible" by Dave Majumdar – April 13, 2015.

103 *Guardianlv.com* "Argentina to Host Russian Bases While America Sleeps" by Jerry Nelson – March 25, 2014.

The Cost to the American People and Innocent Deaths Worldwide that Will Result from Obama's U.N.-Inspired Foreign Policy Decisions

1. The National Security Interest and Economic Cost to the American People

First, instead of conducting U.S. foreign Policy driven by his sworn responsibility to act in the best National Security interests of the American People, President Obama chose to effectively adopt and implement United Nations Multinational policy in virtually all matters and issues pertaining to U.S. foreign policy. Specifically, in all foreign policy matters – ranging from 1) Climate Change, 2) Lax Border Security and Immigration policy, 3) Closing Guantanamo Bay, 4) U.S. Target-Strike Policy that unduly restricts the U.S. military in the War against ISIS, 5) The Iran Nuclear Deal to 6) Ending the Trade Embargo against Cuba – President Obama is 100% in lockstep agreement with United Nations policy.

In stark contrast, while ingratiating himself with the United Nations Secretary-General Ban Ki-moon's priority worldview of Global Governance, Mr. Obama is doing so at the expense of the American People on those very issues that a vast majority have opposed throughout his Presidency (typically by 2 to 1 margins according to opinion polls), as follows:

Issue	Opinion Response
1. Climate Change (If it meant utility prices would have to increase by 10%)	Opposed: 68% to 29% (Also Opposed by Democrats: 56% to 41%)
2. Keystone XL Pipeline	Approve: 63% to 37%
3. Immigration (Worried/Not Worried)	Worried: 63% to 16%
4. U.S. Border Security (Get it under Control)	Control it: 93% to 7%
5. The Guantanamo Bay Terrorist Prison Facility	Keep it Open: 66% to 29%
6. U.S. Drone Policy Against ISIS	Unrestricted Use: 71% to 22%
7. ISIS Threat: President Obama's Performance?	Disapprove: 61% to 38%
8. A) The Iran Nuclear Deal B) The Iran Nuclear Deal (Will Iran cheat regardless?)	Opposed: 59% to 25% Yes: 71%
9. End the Economic Embargo against Cuba (Without Cuba first conceding to A) begin holding free elections and B) move towards a free economy)	No: 50% to 43%

Second, as a consequence, by prioritizing the implementation of United Nations policy in the conduct of U.S foreign policy (in opposition to the will of a clear majority of the American People, according to the above opinion polls), Barack Obama has demonstrably failed the American People – subordinating their optimal National and Economic Security – and, thus disregarding his primary responsibility and oath to serve their best interests and those of the country first and foremost. Specifically:

1. **The Iran Nuclear Deal:** In the interest of peace at any cost, in effect, President Obama (and the United Nations) is permitting i.e. legally sanctioning the right of Iran to permanently obtain and possess nuclear weapons within 10-15 years. It has been widely suggested that Barack Obama's zeal to strike any deal with the Iranians is driven primarily by his desperation and ambition to consummate, what he believes, would be the signature foreign policy Presidential legacy achievement of his Presidency (Chapter 8).

2. **Illegal Immigration and Border Security:** Sacrificing Border Security and failing to prioritize the overhaul of a lax judicial deportation system to vastly expedite the adjudication process (Chapter 5). As a consequence, based on a report released by the House Judiciary Committee (written by the nonpartisan Congressional Research Service), during the three-year period from October 2008-July 2011, 46,000 illegal immigrants with serious felony records were subsequently released by federal law enforcement. However, while awaiting deportation proceedings, of the 46,000 criminal illegal aliens released,

19 murders and 3 attempted murders were committed in addition to 142 sex crimes.

"President Obama's reckless amnesty agenda is dangerous and deadly for Americans. Rather than protect the American People he was elected to protect and serve, President Obama has imposed a policy that allows thousands of illegal immigrants to be released into our communities…President Obama continues to further his anti-enforcement agenda while innocent Americans suffer the consequences. His unwillingness to enforce Immigration laws puts our communities at risk and cost American lives."

Lamar Smith (R-TX), U.S. House Judiciary Committee Chairman – July 31, 2012[104]

The latest victim: The fatal shooting of Kate Steinle in the "sanctuary city" of San Francisco by a criminal alien. President Obama, given his total silence on the purposeful disregard of U.S. immigration law by sanctuary cities, in effect, condones the policy which fosters a collective flagrant flouting of U.S. Federal Immigration law by the more than 200 sanctuary cities across the United States.

3. **War against ISIS:** Obama's refusal to ramp up the U.S. military commitment – in terms of airborne attacks and U.S. troops - to the requisite level necessary to defeat the terrorist threat from ISIS (Chapter 7).

4. **4. Closing GTMO - Lowering the National Security Bar:** Based upon a recent relaxation and less stringent interpretation and subjective judgment of the likelihood of terrorist detainees "returning to the battlefield" (i.e. the

recidivism rate), the Obama Administration has been cava-lierly, if not recklessly, accelerating the release of GTMO terrorist detainees for the principal purpose of reducing the prison population below an arbitrary minimum num-ber that would eventually justify its closing. Illustratively, one contributing factor being promoted to justify recent detainee releases is that, now 10+ years later, terrorist de-tainees are arbitrarily and subjectively judged to be "too old" to "return to the battlefield." However, in doing so, the recidivism rate will inevitably rise – to the detriment of the National Security of the American People - if for no other reason than due to the incremental number of ter-rorists detainees that, under the relaxed National Security subjective interpretation and judgment evaluation process, have already been released or will be in the future, who would otherwise not have qualified in the past (Chapter 6).

5.   **Climate Change:** The imposition of Billions of dollars in new taxes on the American People every year (i.e. a projected $200 Billion, or a 10% increase in 2014 alone) to pay for compliance with new Climate Change-inspired EPA government regulations; also at the expense of max-imizing the American economic recovery (Chapter 3).

2.   The Inevitability of Innocent Civilian Deaths Worldwide

A.   Thousands of Incremental Innocent Civilian Deaths Caused by ISIS

What of the tens of thousands of innocent civilian Iraqis and Syrians who have died or, inevitably will die during the last

two years of his Presidency because Barack Obama refuses to immediately commit the U.S. military to the requisite troop build-up and unhampered military strike capability necessary to defeat the ISIS threat, as urged by even the United Nations (Chapter 7). Indeed, according to United Nations Resolution 2170 (2014), "the 15-member Security Counsel stressed that (ISIS) must be defeated and that the intolerance, violence and hatred it espouses must be stamped out."

As a consequence, certainly neither the United Nations, nor specifically even Russia or China are standing in the way, holding President Obama back from this just cause in doing everything within his power immediately, as President of the United States, to eradicate ISIS.[105] Further, if he were to ramp up the U.S. military effort to defeat ISIS, with the United Nations having specifically endorsed the call for military action against ISIS, one would think that President Obama has nothing either to fear in terms of criticism that, in any way, could harm any potential political chance of him becoming the U.N. Secretary-General one day.

Although, hopefully Mr. Obama's reticence is not born out of a hyper-concern about tarnishing his meticulously crafted image as a world peacemaker who, above all, "was elected to end two wars - not start them." **However, if it is, how brazenly self-consumed would someone have to be to stand by and accept the tens of thousands of incremental innocent civilian Iraqi and Syrian lives that will inevitably continue to be lost over the last two years of the Obama Presidency** because of a perceived risk to one's legacy image - from either:

1. Getting bogged down in a war that may not end before President Obama leaves office and/or

2. Obama's fear that unintentional collateral deaths of innocent civilians from airborne attacks may engender further criticism and charges of human rights violations from the United Nations.

And, if neither is a legitimate concern of President Obama, why, in only this singular instance, doesn't President Obama want to do what even the United Nations, Russia, China and Pope Francis agree and want to see done?

B. Asylum for Christian Refugees Who Fled ISIS in 2014-2015

Specifically regarding his concern about international human rights violations, why won't President Obama even consider providing asylum in the United States to the more than 160,000 Middle East Christians currently languishing in refugee camps, who were uprooted from their homes and religiously persecuted (or living in fear of being persecuted) by ISIS for refusing to convert to Islam? From the perspective of international human rights as promulgated by United Nation policy (for which Mr. Obama discernably has repeatedly demonstrated an affinity for throughout his Presidency), it is baffling as to how or why President Obama would deny consideration of asylum for the 160,000 Middle East Christians who Pope Francis has declared are obvious victims of religious persecution – which, indeed, would specifically qualify them for asylum and residence status in the United States. Especially given that President Obama's tepid response thus far to the War against ISIS virtually guarantees that there will be no relief or resolution for years to come that will allow these Christian refugees to one day return to their homelands in peace.

Yet, Mr. Obama balks, showing little or no enthusiasm while, at the same time, pleading the humanitarian case for taking in the tens of thousands of illegal immigrants fleeing Central American countries because of domestic drug and/or gang violence - even though fleeing from domestic drug and/or gang violence, under current United States Immigration law, is not a valid justification for granting asylum protection. Specifically, current U.S. Immigration law only grants asylum consideration for immigrants fleeing from political, ethnic or religious persecution – not internal drug and/or gang violence that flourishes because of inadequate domestic law enforcement efforts in their respective native countries. **Thus, juxtaposed against his rationale for accepting refugees from Central America, the Middle East Christian refugees - persecuted because of their religious beliefs - have an even stronger legal rationale in qualifying for asylum in the United States as a basis for applying for resident status than Mr. Obama's already established clear preference and commitment for accepting only Central American refugees.**

First, as to his rationale, certainly Mr. Obama isn't suggesting that illegal immigrants from Central America should get preferential treatment over persecuted Middle East refugees simply because they are already here – i.e. that the Middle East Christian refugees cannot provide for their own transportation and, therefore should be denied. Note that the Obama Administration is more than willing to pick up the tab for resettling Syrian refugees - flying them in from the Middle East.

Second, the Obama Administration cannot hide behind the 75,000 per year limit on refugee immigrants entering this country either. To wit, President Obama had no qualms about shattering that ceiling with the very admission of at least an additional 60,000 children in 2014 alone (according to Administration estimates) who entered this country illegally with President Obama's blessing to stay essentially forever.

Finally, one would hope that a President who sees all the nations and the people of the world as equals, would not allow himself to be driven by petty political self-interest to deprive the 160,000 Middle East Christian refugees of residence status in this country because the issue might draw further undo negative attention and reignite debate in the United States as to Mr. Obama's unpopular insistence (consistent with that of the United Nations) that the motivation of ISIS, somehow, has nothing to do with religion.

And if the motivation of President Obama's failure to immediately consider the plight of these 160,000 persecuted Christian refugees is not for the reasons cited above, how can he, in good conscience, continue to only justify his endorsement to effectively grant asylum and admission to the tens of thousands of illegal immigrant children from Central America? Lastly, if none of the reasons cited above is plausible and/or the pretext as to why President Obama cannot or will not support granting refugee status for these 160,000 persecuted Middle East Christians, as President, Mr. Obama owes the American People and those Christian refugees an explanation as to why - and the Media has a moral obligation, if not at least the journalistic curiosity (one would hope) to ask him. Reiterating, hopefully, his refusal to grant Syrian and Iraqi Christian refugees asylum on religious grounds is more than just Barack Obama elevating his own self-interest of avoiding having to revisit and further highlight his unpopular contention that Radical Islamic Terrorism has nothing to do with religion. Although, if the President and his State Department still won't say it, now (12/29/2015) even the presumptive 2016 Democrat Presidential Nominee Hillary Clinton – like Pope

Francis – acknowledges that the killing of thousands of Christians by ISIS thus far clearly amounts to religious genocide.

Yet Syrian Muslim Refugees Get Immediate Priority Asylum Consideration

> "Secretary-General Ban Ki-moon's Special Representative on Migration (Peter Sutherland) says it's 'not enough' for countries like the United States and wealthy Persian Gulf states to give money to help Syrian refugees – they must take them too. 'Buying your way out of this is not satisfactory.'"[106]

Again, taking the cue directly from the United Nations almost immediately (i.e. this time within just 48 hours after Sutherland's pronouncement on September 8, 2015), President Obama's White House Press Secretary Josh Ernest announced the initial intention to take in 10,000 Syrian Muslim refugees in 2016; subsequently upping that number to what could be as many as 200,000 over the next two years. And although the United Nations summarily eschews and admonishes the National Security immigrant concerns of U.N. member states, it is simply a fact that it will be virtually impossible to ferret out terrorist and ISIS elements seeking asylum in Europe or the United States who show up with either A) absolutely no identification or B) forged Syrian passport forms reportedly stolen by the hundreds from the Syrian government. In fact, ISIS had previously vowed to infiltrate the United States precisely in this manner - under the cover of the hundreds of thousands of refugees fleeing Syria in 2015.

Most importantly, FBI Director James Comey contends that it would be impossible today to vet the National Security threat posed by the tens of thousands of refugees scheduled over the next two years to enter the United States. Nevertheless the United Nations has spoken and, consequently, President Obama remains defiant about his intention to admit 10,000 refugees from Syria in 2016 – no matter the threat to National Security.

By contrast, from purely a National Security perspective, the vast majority of the 160,000 Christians, who 1) have already been in Middle East refugee camps for well over a year now and 2) have legitimate documentation of their identification that can be practicably vetted, are ignored by the Obama Administration and left to languish in limbo. Moreover, President Obama needs to justifiably answer why it is fair that those 160,000 Middle East Christians currently relegated to live in refugee camps for well over a year must now also stand behind the apparent priority status given to predominantly Muslim Syrian refugees for immediate admittance and who only recently (mid-2015) began fleeing their homeland by the hundreds of thousands.

The difference: Although U.N. Special Representative Sutherland does not dispute Christian refugees are also "entitled to be given sanctuary," the United Nations has never specifically "called out" the United States; publically advocating that it similarly grant asylum on behalf of Middle East Christian refugees. And unless the United Nations were to, Barack Obama has no incentive to act (i.e. placate the U.N.).

Consequently, although sadly ironic, for those organizations representing Christian refugees, their time probably would have been better spent focusing their appeals directly to Barack Obama's mentor U.N. Secretary-General Ban Ki-moon, if they truly want to get Barack Obama's attention.

CHAPTER 10

104 1) *Washington Times* "Report Cites Killings Blamed on Non-Deported Illegals" by Stephen Dinan – July 31, 2012. 2) *The Blaze* "Report: Illegal Aliens Released by Federal Gov't Committed 19 murders, 142 Sex Crimes" by Jason Howerton – July 31, 2012.

105 Of course, candidly, from the perspective of both Russia and China, why not let the United States repeatedly expend only their blood and treasure to rid the world of the ISIS threat.

106 *Associated Press* "The Latest: Israel Blames Migrant Crisis on Militant Islam" – September 8, 2015.

Charting the Optimal Strategy for Barack Obama to Insure One Day Becoming the U.N. Secretary-General

To Barack Obama, a President of the United States retiring after two terms, having won the Nobel Peace Prize and becoming the U.N. Secretary-General one day would, in world history, be an unprecedented level of achievement and crowning Presidential legacy.

Barack Obama does have an ego, as do all of us. However, only if uncheck is an ego a bad thing that, to excess, can become to varying degrees narcissistic, self-serving and/or blind one's objectivity. In a positive sense, our egos are the mental engine upon which we draw to pursue accomplishment – be it financial, political, or altruistic or a combination of all three – driven hopefully by our compassion, intellect, internal fortitude, vigilance and determination. Combined with his gift of oratory and enthusiastic preference for appearing before like-minded audiences, it would seem that Barack Obama's temperament would, indeed, be the perfect fit to become United Nations Secretary-General.

Further, having proactively rejected, throughout his Presidency 1) the concept of U.S. Exceptionalism by 2) promoting a diminished role for the United States as the dominant player in world affairs,

President Obama is conversely consciously serving the cause of raising the stature of the United Nations as the true heir to, what world body truly believes is its rightful and exclusive priority role in heading global governance in the 21ˢᵗ Century. Simultaneously, his efforts as President of the United States – by conducting U.S. foreign policy in the mirror-image of United Nations dogma - will further serve as a prelude for which Barack Obama would also benefit in an enhanced way as a future Secretary-General of the United Nations.

Granting him the benefit of doubt, perhaps Barack Obama believes that 1) through Multinational global governance truly led by the United Nations and 2) the correspondingly diminished role in foreign affairs that the United States would assume as a result, this country will, nevertheless collaterally achieve the realization of what is in its own best National Security interest anyway. Beyond that, if the United States is also relegated to endure a just comeuppance for past transgressions and arrogant superpower hegemony (e.g. Obama: "America has acted unilaterally, without regard for the interests of others") along the way – so much the better.

The Optimal Strategy:

1. **Cultivating the Support and Endorsement of both Kofi Annan and Ban Ki-moon**

   "President Obama has already demonstrated a commitment to a nuclear free world, to international cooperation, to respect of the rule of [international] law, and has joined the fight against Climate Change. He has shown that the only way forward is through genuine cooperation with other nations."

Kofi Annan, then-former UN Secretary-General - The Kofi
Annan Foundation – October 2009

Reiterating, even before the 2008 Presidential election, Annan, the
first Black United Nations Secretary-General, was most enthusiastic about Barack Obama winning - stating that the prospect of an
Obama Presidency would be "phenomenal."[107]

Similarly, note the highest of praise for Barack Obama from Ban
Ki-moon:

> *"We are entering an era of renewed Multinationalism, a
> new era where President Obama has brought a new vision
> of a world based on human decency, fairness and freedom,
> which is an inspiration to challenge us all facing humankind
> who demand global common cause and uncommon global
> effort. President Obama embodies the new spirit of dialogue
> and engagement on the world's biggest problems: Climate
> Change, nuclear disarmament and a wide range of peace
> and security challenges."*
> Ban Ki-moon, U.N. Secretary-General – October 9, 2009

Sounds like, at least in the minds of Kofi Annan and Ban Ki-moon,
Barack Obama has checked off all the right boxes. Secondly, Barack
Obama's ascension to the position of United Nations Secretary-
General at some point would (it is hoped) further commensurately
raise the dominant profile of the United Nations on the world
stage. Indeed, it is simply a recognition of fact that, since the in-
ception of the United Nations 70 years ago, the dominant shadow
of the sway that the United States has held in world affairs has
effectively stunted the authority and image, as perceived by U.N.
advocates, of the global body's rightful dominant and exclusive

role in promoting world leadership achieved through true global governance based on Multinationalism.

Lastly, note that the very next day after Ban Ki-moon had announced his candidacy (in 2011) to serve for a second term as U.N. Secretary-General, President Barack Obama, like any devoted disciple, announced his unqualified glowing support: *"Under Ban's leadership, the United Nations has played a critical role in responding to crises and challenges across the globe..."*[108] Similarly, in the interim under the term of Antonio Guterres as U.N. Secretary-General, Barack Obama would further benefit by making himself available to serve when called upon, perhaps, in the capacity of a Special Envoy to the United Nations in peace-keeping efforts.

It could be said that, since becoming a Presidential candidate in 2007, Barack Obama's actions and intentions - as demonstrated by incessantly placating the wishes and promoting the political policy positions held by United Nations Secretary-General Ban Ki moon and his predecessor Kofi Annan - are consistent with and really not unlike the analogy of the quintessential corporate "Yes man" underling who, at every turn, emulates and parrots the goals and objectives of his boss in hopes of, one day, taking over his job after he retires. The only distinction here is that a corporate "Yes man" is not bound by an exclusive superseding sworn moral and legal obligation to – first and foremost – serve the optimal National Security interests of the American People.

Ultimately, virtually every foreign policy decision made by Barack Obama throughout his first seven years as President of the United States, couldn't have emulated more the Multinational geo-political worldview and ideological thrust of the United Nations than if

President Obama had been, in effect, purposely auditioning all along to become the next Secretary-General of the United Nations in 2017.

2. Throughout his Presidency, Barack Obama adopted the U.N. Multinationalism Policy Almost Verbatim

Indeed, a comparative analysis of the code-worded language and phrases in U.N. speeches and policy statements revealed the striking similarity and joint purpose between those words spoken over the years by President Obama on specific foreign policy issues and his counterparts at the United Nations, Ban Ki-moon and Kofi Annan – who have served as the current and former U.N. Secretaries-General respectively for nearly the last two decades (see Chapter 3). In particular, an analysis of the following issues focused specifically upon that comparison of similar, sometimes almost verbatim use of terms and phrases by Barack Obama and those espoused by the U.N. Secretaries-General in underscoring their joint preference for and promotion of Multinational global governance:

A. **Illegal Immigration:** If widely known, it would be shocking to most Americans to find out that the United Nations adamantly discards, outright, any and all National Security concerns of member nations – instead opting to promote a free migration policy reflecting an almost utopian open borders philosophy among nations. **Specifically, the language that appears in U.N. policy statements and speeches regarding the issues of downplaying Border Control and National Security is pure Multinational worldview rhetoric in tone; subjectively colored by a reflection of a theoretical rather than a "real world" view; which is naïve almost to the point of being reckless** (i.e. Paragraphs

56, 57 and 59; of the U.N. report delivered on August 7, 2014 by Ban Ki-moon entitled "Promotion and Protection of Human Rights...of Migrants" – at International Borders-see Chapter 5). By his own words, President Obama as well, sympathetically exemplifies his support for the primary tenet espoused by the United Nations that immigrants who cross international borders without permission have not even committed a crime – when he intimates that the U.S. should instead focus on *"Felons, not families. Criminals, not children."*

Finally, it has been estimated that anywhere from 42% to 45% of the total number of illegal immigrants in the United States emanate from individuals who overstayed their visas and ultimately illegally chose not to leave the country. Consequently, the illegal immigration problem in this country could be cut virtually in half by just hunting down each one of these illegal immigrants and deporting them.

Why wouldn't President Obama – and every citizen concerned about the best National Security Interest of the American People – support legislation to increase Homeland Security budgeting, whatever the cost, to hire the requisite number of agents to track down and deport all immigrant "over-stays" who have illegally refused to leave this country? What defense could President Obama present for immigrants who have illegally overstayed their visas? There is none. What plausible explanation or rationale could President Obama – whose sworn priority is to insure the optimal National Security Interest of the American People – have to be against such a proposal? Although, for President Obama to support such a proposal would be in total contradiction with the U.N. "Open Borders" International Immigration policy ultimately codified in 2014 (Paragraph 59). And, if such legislation were passed, the United Nations no doubt would be disappointed, to say the least, if President Obama didn't do everything within his power, including his veto, to stand in the way.

B. **Islamic Extremism vs. Violent Extremism:** In February 2015, President Obama was still declining to use the term "Islamic Terrorism" (as does the United Nations) even in the aftermath of terrorist attacks in Paris by self-proclaimed Muslims shouting "Allahu akbar," while in the act of committing their atrocities against Jewish journalists at the newspaper Charles Hebdo and a Jewish-delicatessen, killing 17 in all (Chapter 4).

Compare the following statements of then-U.N. Secretary-General Kofi Annan and President Obama as an illustration concerning their dual contention that typically religiously-inspired conflicts are, in fact, *not* rooted in religion at all. First Kofi Annan:

"Some of the conflicts we are seeing – believing that it is religion which is at the basis, is not necessarily so. Most of it is political policies and differences, which pushes some people sometimes to take the law into their own hands and go in another direction. The issue is not faith."
Kofi Annan, then-U.N. Secretary-General – December 19, 2006

Compared to Barack Obama:

"We must never accept the premise that they [ISIS] put

*forward because it is a lie. Nor should we grant these ter-rorists the legitimacy that they seek. **They are not religious leaders. They are terrorists.***"
President Barack Obama – February 18, 2015 at the White House Summit on Countering "Violent Extremism"

C. Global Governance: Regarding President Barack Obama's resolute adoption of the United Nations Multinational Global Governance philosophy, compare Annan:

"No nation can make itself secure by seeking supremacy over all others." -
Kofi Annan, then-U.N. Secretary-General – December 11, 2006

To Obama:

"No one nation can or should try to dominate another na-tion. No world order that elevates one nation or a group of nations over another will succeed."
President Barack Obama – September 29, 2009

Given the near verbatim use of words and intent by both men, in President Obama's inaugural speech before the United Nations General Assembly on September 29, 2009, it was as if the President's political handlers and speech writers had then-U.N. Secretary-General Kofi Annan's December 11, 2006 U.N. Farewell speech in hand when the above quote was penciled into Mr. Obama's speech.

Indeed, if one can paraphrase and parrot "right back at them" the thoughts and words of others with whom

one desires to ingratiate himself, so much the better. Is that not also the sincerest form of political flattery? It is almost as if President Obama's speech writers downloaded and "fly-specked" virtually every speech made by Secretaries-General Ban Ki-moon and Kofi Annan with the specific intent being to paraphrase and insert selected quotes of both men sprinkled into the foreign policy speeches of President Obama throughout his presidency.

Alternatively, as further demonstrative evidence as to President Obama's lockstep and unquestioned adherence to the substitution and implementation of United Nations policy for American foreign policy, take note of the rapidity with which Mr. Obama changed course (i.e. "got back into line") to comply and comport with United Nations criticism of the United States, *which occurred publically only twice* during his Presidency:

1. President Obama's intention of bombing Syria for using chemical weapons in September 2013 – *Within just two weeks,* President Obama backed off his "red line" promise; opting instead for a Russian-brokered deal for Assad's promise to give up all of his chemical weapons arsenal (which the Syrian Government *has not yet done* to this very day). Specifically, U.N. Secretary-General Ban Ki-moon admonished the United States that to execute a "punitive" military strike against Syria, *without prior approval from the United Nations Security Council* would also be a violation of international law. To wit, a military response by one nation against another (without prior U.N. approval) is only permissible in self-defense (i.e. Article 51 of the United Nations Charter).

2. In May 2013, President Obama instituted a revised

U.S. Drone and Military Strike-Targeting policy implementing such severe targeting approval restriction criteria that U.S. aircraft military strikes have been effectively reduced by more than 75 percent in the War against ISIS in Iraq. **However, note that this Strike-targeting policy change was instituted by President Obama *just two months after* United Nations Special Envoy on Human Rights and Counter-Terrorism Ben Emmerson had declared the United States to be in violation of international human law** for failing to gain prior consent from the host nation (in this case, Pakistan) before launching drone strikes.

D. **Nuclear Non-Proliferation and Climate Change:** Similarly, regarding the United Nations priority issue of Nuclear Non-Proliferation - specifically, 1) the Nuclear Non-Proliferation Treaty and 2) the Comprehensive Nuclear-Test-Ban Treaty - note the near-verbatim use of code words and phrases in speeches by Barack Obama (see introductory pages to Chapter 8). Likewise, regarding the current Number One Priority of the United Nations, Climate Change, see Chapter 3.

3. **Politically Crafting Barack Obama's Presidential Foreign Policy Credentials and Image**

The promotion of foreign policy achievement throughout Barack Obama's Presidency has always been at the forefront of both Mr. Obama and his political advisors - interwoven simultaneously with continually demonstrating, through his actions, a strict adoption of, adherence to and tenacity for applying United Nations Multinational policy in the conduct of U.S. foreign policy. Second, from virtually the beginning of his Presidency, with the rejection of advice from

European leaders Andrea Merkel and Nicholas Sarkozy to confront Iran at the United Nations in 2009 with evidence of their secret weapons-grade nuclear facility, Barack Obama's own cultivated political image as a *non-confrontational* world peacemaker has always taken precedence.

Even lauded investigative reporter and author Bob Woodward (*Obama's Wars* - Copyright 2010) characterized the Obama White House staff as being totally preoccupied by political ramifications, which dominated the entire Presidential decision-making process:[109]

> "It's political. They (the White House staff) immediately think, 'What's the political impact?'...It's a permanent campaign.'"

Although Woodward, who was given unprecedented singular access to cover the White House in writing the book he was promoting (*Obama Wars)*, hastened to add his belief that President Obama, unlike his White House staff, is not politically preoccupied. However, it is President Obama who is responsible for picking his White House staff and, just as importantly, setting the tone that allowed political impact considerations to dominate and consume the thinking among his advisors during his Presidency (One doubts that Woodward would be so forgiving to Richard Nixon as to the responsibility he bore for the actions of his White House staff and advisors during Watergate).

4. The Multinational "Takedown" of America: Theme and Purpose

On the surface, some may consider the word, *Takedown* appearing in the title of this book as being too harsh or "over the top."

However, considering the dictionary definition, the word *Takedown* has proven to be entirely fitting:

> *Takedown: An instance of humiliation; an instance of making somebody* (or in this case a nation, according to Obama) *less arrogant or powerful.*[110]

Indeed, less than three months after taking office (April 2, 2009), President Obama admonished America, stating that this country has *"shown arrogance and been dismissive, even derisive."* As further demonstrative evidence of his lockstep adoption of United Nations Multinational philosophy, within five months of his inauguration in 2009, President Obama had begun what many critics had termed an "Apology Tour" – to "take down" America. Specifically, President Obama visited capitals around the world proclaiming that in the past, the United States was, in effect, guilty as charged by its critics as to conducting foreign policy exclusively in its own best interest - without the slightest consideration for the security and wellbeing of the international community of nations. And throughout his Presidency, Barack Obama has continued to frequently admonish his own country in this manner.

5. Continually Pandering to U.N. Muslim States

Similarly, whether President Obama is repeatedly 1) insisting (from his Christian perspective) that Muslim terrorist groups really don't believe in Islam (i.e. in denying the authenticity of their literal interpretation of the Koran- Chapter 4) to 2) never missing an opportunity to prematurely leap to the microphones when there is even a hint or mere possibility that heinous atrocities may have been committed against Muslims because of their faith (e.g. The three Muslim students murdered in North Carolina – Chapter 9), **Barack Obama is**

attempting to convey to the Muslim World that – unlike their negative perception of America and its people – he is separate and distinct in all ways; being at the forefront of promoting and protecting, in particular, the rights and interests of all Muslim nation states worldwide and their people.

Indeed, Barack Obama knows full-well that it is a given he must have the crucial support and votes of the U.N. Muslim states should he ever want to become the United Nations Secretary-General. Moreover, note that it was President Obama alone who hastened to downplay any Muslim terrorist involvement as exemplified in 1) the so-called Fort Hood shootings (November 2009), labelled, rather, by the Obama Administration as "domestic workplace violence" (even though U.S. Army Sgt. Nidal Hasan was shouting "Allahu akbar" while committing his murderous rampage) or 2) the "Underwear bomber" over Detroit (December 2009). Ultimately, however, both incidents have since been clearly shown to have had "Al-Qaida in Yemen" connections and direction.

Above all, so long as Barack Obama remains as President, there will be no ramping up of the coalition military commitment to requisite levels necessary in an all-out effort to defeat ISIS. Short of a major terrorist attack on American soil, to do otherwise would, from President Obama's perspective, be totally incongruous and negate all his efforts to assuage the Muslim world of nations throughout his Presidency.

Further note that *there is no other answer to every one of the following questions than the one proffered herein* that would explain

President Obama's principal rationale and behavior in his conduct of U.S. foreign policy throughout his Presidency – i.e. Barack Obama's desire to possibly one day become the U.N. Secretary-General by pandering to and placating U.N. leaders and Muslim nations.

Regarding any other possible Presidential rationale that might encompass a plausible explanation for the following U.S. foreign policy actions, many (even including Obama acolytes) were left to wonder at times "Where might he be coming from?" or, simply muttering, "Huh?" Moreover, there was absolutely no domestic political value (i.e. "upside") to President Obama's actions and positions taken with respect to every one of the following questions listed below that would explain his motivation:

1. **Pandering to Muslims:** Why would President Obama "go public" in opposition to the description of America as built on a Judeo-Christian ethic – proclaiming, rather, that the United States is neither a Christian, Jewish or Muslim nation? (June 2009)

2. **Pandering to Muslims:** Why would President Obama insist and advise his Director of NASA to accentuate and extol the virtues of Muslim scientific achievement as his *Number One priority* at the Space Agency? (July 2010)

3. **Pandering to Muslims:** Why would President Obama purposely inject himself into a controversy that his Administration had earlier stated was a "local issue;" by later personally pronouncing support for the construction of the Ground Zero Mosque in lower Manhattan? (August 2010)

4. **Climate Change:** Why would President Obama publically

state his specific intention to effectively close down most coal-fired energy plants nationwide through legislative measures and EPA regulation and, thus as a necessary consequence of his action, substantially increase utility costs for all Americans? (Chapter 3)

5. **Re: Islamic Extremism vs. Violent Extremism - Verbatim Adoption of U.N. Policy:** Even many Democrats wondered why President Obama would not use the term, *Islamic Extremism*, when Pope Francis (in describing the 2015 beheadings of 21 Egyptian Coptic Christians) and the French Government (i.e. the 17 people killed in the 2015 Paris terrorist attacks on Jewish Journalists at Charlie Hebdo and a Jewish-delicatessen) freely characterized it as Islamic terrorism based upon the obvious religious beliefs of the perpetrators (i.e. Islam) and those of the Jewish victims that they targeted? (Chapter 4)

6. **U.S. Amnesty for Illegals Mirrors Extreme/Recklessly-Naive U.N. Immigration Policy:** Given that overwhelmingly A) by a 63% to 16% margin the American People are deeply concerned about illegal immigration and B) by a 93% to 7% margin the American People stress the National Security importance of securing the U.S. border, why would President Obama cavalierly choose to continually ignore their National Security concerns about terrorism? (Chapter 5)

7. **Obama's Lockstep Adherence to U.N. Policy:** Probably President Obama's greatest foreign policy failure and humiliation (inviting criticism from even from his former Defense Secretary) occurred when he vehemently vowed to punitively punish Syria and President Assad for killing

1,400 innocent civilians with chemical weapons - but only days later changed his mind. Remember: Moreover, it was President Obama who declared that it was not in the National Security interests of the United States to ignore the Syrian chemical attack. However, it was hardly mere coincidence that the timing of President Obama's withdrawal of his "red line" promise occurred just 7 days after U.N. Secretary-General Ban Ki-moon publically warned that, to punitively strike Syria without prior approval from the U.N. Security Council would also be a violation of international law. And today: What about the numerous chemical weapons attacks by the Syrian Government that have occurred since August 2013? (Chapter 7)

8. **Closing GTMO:** When only 1 in 3 Americans with opinions, have consistently supported his determination to close the Guantanamo Bay prison facility, why would President Obama continue "relentless" and undeterred to close it down - disregarding, out of hand, what an overwhelming majority of the American People believe is a National Security threat in the President's expediting the release of known Jihadi terrorists? (Chapter 6)

9. **Obama and the U.N. Legally Sanction Iran's Right to Become a Nuclear Weapons Power:** Where opinion polls reveal that only 1 in 4 Americans approve of the 2015 Iran Nuclear Deal, (as simply and succinctly stated by Rush Limbaugh[111]) "why would Obama want Iran to have nukes" ever - in clear violation and outright nullification of the 45 year-old Nuclear Non-Proliferation Treaty which has now been rendered meaningless? (Chapter 8)

10. **Admitting Tens of Thousands of Syrian Refugees into the U.S.:** At extreme risk to U.S. National Security - why would President Obama have caved - within 48 hours - to United Nations criticism as to the United States' responsibility to accept tens of thousands of Syrian refugees? Notwithstanding the declarations of the Intelligence community and, no less than FBI Director James Comey that there currently isn't any assurance that the U.S. can adequately identify and screen out elements of ISIS and related terrorist affiliates hidden among those who are legitimate Syrian refugees.

"National Security is not a privilege or an option. National Security is a right that the President must understand is his first and most important priority… There are all too many people in academia and global business that aren't really interested in America as a nation-state anymore. They're interested in building a different global order that will protect their economic interest and philosophical interest. Not in building a strong America that will protect the American Interest."
Governor Chris Christie, 2016 Republican Presidential Candidate – November 15, 2015.

This book is written for those American People with an open-mind and who may actually care whether, in fact, they were deceived by Barack Obama once again, in never candidly "leveling" with them - be it Obamacare (during the 2012 Presidential election) or in this case, his unquestioned devotion to the United Nations Multinational form of Global Governance. **Specifically, Barack Obama, by his actions as President, purposely chose 1) to give priority consideration to the goals and objectives of the United**

Nations in conducting U.S. foreign policy (The Obama Doctrine of "Leading from Behind") above the optimal National Security interests of the American People while, simultaneously 2) advancing his own personal and political legacy ambition should he wish one day to become the Secretary-General of the United Nations.

Most assuredly, this book will be considered an anathema to the hardcore 35%-42% of Liberal Democrat acolytes who – short of treason or murder – will always be there, anytime, anywhere, to support and vote for Barack Obama or Hillary Clinton no matter what. Indeed, illustrative of their unflinching allegiance to the Democrat Party and outright distain for Republicans, alternatively, these Democrats do not care in the least that, for example, President Obama had to purposely lie to the American People to insure the enactment of Obamacare into law and its preservation which, in doing so, secured his own re-election as President (whereas he would otherwise have lost, according to opinion polls).

Metaphorically, the phrase "a pane of glass," in terms of describing human behavior, "implies an unmasking of intention, of the hidden becoming visible; you can see the obvious intentions of their action, often self-serving in nature."[112]

Convincingly, the most telling confirmation of Barack Obama's total adoption and adherence to the United Nations Multinational form of Global Governance is demonstrated simply by his actions in conducting U.S. foreign policy over the last seven years. Indeed, one might counterintuitively ask: Just what United Nations policy hasn't Barack Obama adopted?[113] Further, as a consequence, collaterally, should he proactively seek to become the Secretary-General of the United Nations one day, Barack Obama, in his conduct of U.S. foreign policy, has optimally laid that groundwork as well.

And, reiterating one last time, had Barack Obama shown the moral courage to have "levelled" with the American People from the outset and revealed that the United Nations model of Global Governance was exactly how he intended to conduct U.S. foreign policy, then there would be no moral question of deceit raised herein (or, for that matter, to have written this book at all). One could readily anticipate Barack Obama to feign Presidential Indignation or counter that it would have been of little or no concern to the American People as to why - from the outset of his candidacy to become President of the United States in 2007 – he never publically and unapologetically advised the American People of his unquestioned reverence for, and intention to conduct U.S. foreign policy deferring predominantly to the goals and objectives, as well as the spirit of the United Nations model of Global Governance.

However, Mr. Obama had to know that politically he could not have levelled with the American People from the outset precisely because of the manner in which he has executed foreign policy as President - juxtaposed against just how contradictory it has proven to be in stark opposition to the political opinions and positions held by a clear majority of the American People throughout his Presidency. Moreover, one needs only to have observed just how Mr. Obama has overtly accelerated the pace of instituting even more controversial foreign policy decisions in just the first five months that immediately followed the final Federal election of his Presidency (November 4, 2014) - which has provided him with even (in his words) "more flexibility" politically to do as he pleases i.e.:

1) Providing U.S. residency status to 4-5 million illegal immigrants (just 10 days after the November 4 Election);

2) President Obama's announcement to resume diplomatic relations with Cuba (December 17, 2014);

3) In January 2015, the Obama Administration formally codified DHS regulations effectively granting amnesty to all illegal immigrants if their only criminal act was illegally entering the U.S. Consequently, "[T]he Obama Administration is on pace to remove 229,000 people from the country (in 2015), a 27% fall from (2014) and 50% less than the all-time high in 2012." (*Washington Post*, July 2, 2015);

4) Reaffirmation to close GTMO (January 20, 2015) and

5) The controversial Iran Nuclear Deal (April 2, 2015).

Barack Obama is nothing if he is not the shrewdest of politicians. In reality, if he was truly not concerned about any negative political impact had the American People knew upfront of his plan to conduct U.S. foreign policy exclusively according to United Nations doctrine, there should have been no reason for Barack Obama to have purposely withheld this intent. Rather, to hail it as a hallmark of U.S foreign policy going forward.

Yet, one must remember President Obama does have a "track record" for purposely withholding his intentions from the American People. Specifically, there have now been at least three documented instances, with the greatest of political and National Security ramifications that occurred during his Presidency, when Barack Obama did, indeed – like a pane of glass - purposely withhold his own self-serving intentions from the American People precisely because of his concern as to their negative reaction if they had, in fact, knew beforehand:

1. Obama's March 2012 secret message meant only for the ears of Russian President Vladimir Putin in proposing yet a further nuclear arms reduction agreement which, obviously, Mr. Obama most certainly did not want the American People to know about before the 2012 Presidential Election.

2. Obama purposely deceiving the American People throughout the 2012 Presidential Campaign by continually assuring them that they would not lose their ability to keep their health plans when, in fact, he knew full well (having acknowledged the fact two years earlier at the 2010 White House Summit on ObamaCare) that millions of Americans, indeed, would.

3. Two months before the 2012 Presidential Election, President Obama and Secretary of State Hillary Clinton collaborated to emphatically and with certitude blame the deaths of four Americans in Benghazi (including the U.S. Ambassador Chris Stevens) on an internet video – even lying to the faces of their relatives, as well as the American People. When, in fact based on documented conversations, Ms. Clinton – within just 24 hours following the attack - had unambiguously informed the Libyan Ambassador, the Prime Minister of Egypt and even her daughter, Chelsea Clinton that the attack had, indeed, been carried out by terrorists associated with Al Qaeda. (e.g. Clinton told the Egyptian Prime Minister: "We know that the attack in Libya had nothing to do with the film. It was a planned attack. Not a protest." September 12, 2012).

    After her testimony to the House Select Committee investigating Benghazi ended (October 22, 2015), a rally was held that evening to claim a political victory for Hillary Clinton over House Republicans which Ms. Clinton triumphantly attended and celebrated with her political operatives. Whereas, rather than celebrating, the relatives of the murdered Benghazi victims who were also present at the hearing that day returned home alone that evening with only their tears. Beyond Ms. Clinton's perceived "political triumph," there was no cause for celebration concerning the murder of these four Americans.

However, just as grave, Barack Obama's conscious lockstep adoption of United Nations policy in conducting U.S. foreign policy - at the expense and in opposition to the will of a decided majority of the American People – has left the National Security of this country in a greater state of peril seven years after he took office. Nevertheless, Barack Obama has worked his will and has purposely and adamantly reasoned, to himself, that he alone knows what is best for the American People more than even they do for themselves. And, like President Obama's secret message meant only for Russian President Putin and the deceptions of Benghazi and Obamacare, in a Machiavellian sense, if deceitfully hiding his true intent from the American People is necessary to accomplish his purpose, so be it.

The Analogy of the Vatican and the United Nations (Revisited)

Finally, in the introductory chapter, specific reference was made to the genuine concern and fear of many American People during the 1960 Presidential campaign, as to whether John F. Kennedy, as President would allow himself to come under the influence and accede to the direction and dictates of the Vatican and the Pope of the Catholic Church – thus, elevating his allegiance to his religion and the Vatican (i.e. a global body and international organization, like the United Nations) above the will and the best interests of the

American People. Similarly, the parallel was specifically drawn herein to President Obama and the question of his lockstep adoption of United Nations policy and his adherence to the political philosophy of Multinationalism and Global Governance – above the best National Security interests and will of the American People (as expressed by a decided majority in issue opinion polls).

However, the analogy ends here. The defining distinction between President John F. Kennedy and President Barack Obama is how each man chose to deal with their respective circumstance: First, unlike President Barack Obama, President John F. Kennedy 1) raised the issue head-on attesting to his overriding allegiance to the American People – and not to that of a world body and international organization (i.e. The Vatican) and 2) chose to do so *before* the 1960 Presidential election. Second, unlike President Obama, President Kennedy, during the course of his Presidency, in fact, never did fashion any aspect of his foreign policy decisions based upon the edicts of the Vatican (i.e. a world body and international organization); never elevating it or his religion above his legal sworn oath and primary responsibility to serve the best National Security interests of the American People, first and foremost.

By contrast, President Barack Obama cannot say the same - as demonstrated by his embracement and lockstep adherence to the edicts and Multinational model of Global Governance espoused by the United Nations (i.e. a world body and international organization) in virtually all aspects of conducting U.S. foreign policy decisions. As a consequence, many times President Obama elevated his preference for it 1) above his sworn highest priority to serve the best National Security interests of the United States and 2) in opposition to the will of a decided majority of the American People as expressed in opinion polls (i.e. Illegal Immigration,

Border Security, Obama's Syrian "Red Line," Closing GTMO, The Iran Nuclear Deal).

Obama's Demonstrative Penchant for U.N. Versus U.S. Foreign Policy

Emblematic of A) the extreme and dangerous divergence between United Nations policy and U.S. foreign policy and B) how President Obama's blind adherence to U.N. policy places U.S. National Security at risk, one need only examine the 2014 United Nations Position Statement on Immigration that, in effect, codified years of inalterable opposition by the United Nations to and total disregard for the National Security interests of member nations. To wit, the 2014 U.N. policy Position Statement on Immigration declares:

1. The National Security concerns expressed by any nation are specious, without foundation and merely used as a pretext by such nations who wish to deny and prevent *the rightful free and unfettered migration of immigrants to any country they wish* to live throughout the world (Paragraphs 56-57).

2. Crossing a border without the approval of the destination country is *not* a violation of any law and the immigrant must be allowed to stay (Paragraph 59). Compared to Obama Administration Actions that mirror the 2014 U.N. Position Statement on Immigration:

   a. Both ICE and the U.S. Citizenship and Immigration Agency ordered federal agents not to detain Illegals if their only violation is illegally entering the United States (since 2011).

b. Through Executive Order, Obama intends to grant amnesty to 4-5 million Illegal Immigrants (2014 – Just four months after the U.N. Position Statement on Immigration was issued).

c. Obama issued a directive ordering that ICE will only enforce U.S. Immigration Law against Illegal Immigrants with Criminal records (i.e. Thus, those Illegals whose only violation is entering the U.S. illegally will not be arrested - 2015).

3. Attempts by a destination country to deport illegal immigrants "can lead to human rights violations and a breach of international principles such as non-refoulement i.e.forcibly returning a refugee to his or her native country" (Paragraph 57).

Compared to Obama Administration Actions that mirror the 2014 U.N. Position Statement on Immigration:

In 2014, the Obama Administration – supported by the United Nations - refused to deport the 60,000+ unaccompanied Illegal Immigrant children who did not qualify for seeking asylum under current U.S. Immigration Law (i.e. claiming they were escaping domestic gang and/or drug violence).

4. Attempts by a destination country to strengthen its border security to prevent illegal entry can also "lead to human rights violations" (Paragraphs 60 and 68).

Compared to Obama Administration Action (and

Inaction) that mirror the 2014 U.N. Position Statement on Immigration:

a. Although having six months' prior warning of the flood of Illegal Immigrant children in 2014, the Obama Administration did nothing to increase border security to prevent their illegal entry into the U.S.

b. Throughout his Presidency, Obama has done little or nothing to 1) increase the requisite number of security personnel (i.e. U.S. Border Control Agents) needed to stem the tide of Illegals crossing the southern border and 2) has refused to accept and deport Illegal Immigrants arrested by state and local law enforcement agencies.

5. "The Convention on the Rights of the Child prescribes that 'no child shall be deprived of his or her liberty unlawfully or arbitrarily (Article 37(b))...(Therefore, Nation) States should expeditiously and completely cease the detention of children on the basis of their migration status'" (Paragraph 21).

Compared to Obama Administration Actions that mirror the 2014 U.N. Position Statement on Immigration:

After The DREAM ACT was voted down by Congress in 2011, then-Secretary of Homeland Security Janet Napolitano - without any statute authority at all - instructed Immigration officers to stop pursuing, prosecuting and deporting illegal immigrants ages 16-30; in naked defiance of U.S. Immigration law.

Indeed, even at the risk of U.S. National Security, President Obama's embracement of the United Nations' 2014 Position Statement on Immigration is the "smoking gun" and the quintessential illustration of his purposeful lockstep adherence to U.N. policy and dictates as demonstrated and evidenced above in his conduct of U.S. foreign policy, as it relates to Illegal Immigration, throughout his Presidency. Moreover, throughout his Presidency, no major policy issue of President Obama has been of more stark concern to the vast majority of the American People (according to issue opinion polls) than his inability - purposeful or not - to control U.S. Border Security i.e. 93% to 7%.

Obama Fails in his National Security Obligation to the American People

Ultimately, although he felt politically compelled to do so, President Kennedy really had no moral obligation to reaffirm to the American People that his primary allegiance was to serve the best National Security interests of the United States - precisely because he never had any intention to conduct U.S. foreign policy primarily guided and influence by the edicts and aspirations of a global body and organization (i.e. The Vatican). **Whereas President Obama - by adopting and elevating the dogma of the United Nations (a global body and organization) in the conduct U.S. foreign policy - had at least the moral obligation to have apprised the American People of his intention to do so at the outset of his candidacy to become President of the United States in 2007. But, unlike President Kennedy, President Obama chose not to.**

And to What End?

As evidenced herein, throughout his Presidency, Barack Obama has demonstrably attempted to fundamentally change and reconstitute the United States of America to more conform to the image of the United Nations precisely by adhering to its dogma, edicts and policies in the conduct of U.S. foreign policy. In doing so, President Obama has arguably and discernably achieved his intent - unless and until the next President of the United States, upon taking office, embarks upon rescinding and dismantling all of Obama's concerted extra-constitutional actions.

Lastly, if President Barack Obama truly has no such political designs to, one day, become United Nations Secretary-General, why wouldn't he be willing to deny it - now - in a Shermanesque-like declaration? Conversely, if he won't, would that not confirm his desire and true intent to leave that option open to, one day, seek the office? Furthermore, if so, as their President, the American People had a right to know - at the outset - that Mr. Obama held the ambition of one day possibly wanting to become the Secretary-General of the United Nations. And had Barack Obama advised the American People of this ambition, the American People would rightfully have had the opportunity to draw their own conclusions, in advance, as to what degree a potential conflict of interest existed, or could occur and to have then decided for themselves and voted accordingly.

CHAPTER 11

107 *Washington Post* "At the U.N., Many Hope for an Obama Win" by Colum Lynch – Ibid - October 26, 2008.

108 *iip.usembassy.gov* "Obama Supports Second Term for U.N.'s Ban Ki-moon" – June 7, 2011.

109 *Larry King Live* – October 3, 2010.

110 Encarta Dictionary: English (North America).

111 *Rush Limbaugh Show (EIB Network)* – September 11, 2015.

112 Ten Millimeters – Metaphor in Life and Art "Metaphors of Transcendence" by Jori Sackin – January 21, 2015.

113 Obama supporters may point to Barack Obama having led the United Nations in the support of the Gay Rights issue which the United Nations only adopted in 2014. However, that issue had previously been repeatedly blocked not by leadership, but institutionally in the U.N. General Assembly over the years by a substantial block of nations whose respective predominant state religion did not support Gay Rights- i.e. primarily Muslim and sub-Saharan Africa nations.